THE BLOODSTAINED FIELD

A History
of the
Sugarloaf Massacre
September 11, 1780

Rogan H. Moore

HERITAGE BOOKS
2007

HERITAGE BOOKS
AN IMPRINT OF HERITAGE BOOKS, INC.

Books, CDs, and more—Worldwide

For our listing of thousands of titles see our website
at
www.HeritageBooks.com

Published 2007 by
HERITAGE BOOKS, INC.
Publishing Division
65 East Main Street
Westminster, Maryland 21157-5026

Copyright © 2000 Rogan H. Moore

Other books by the author:

History and Genealogy of the Moore Families of Fayette County, Pennsylvania
The Civil War Memoirs of Sergeant George W. Darby

International Standard Book Number: 978-0-7884-1488-7

To the People of the

Sugarloaf Valley.

TABLE OF CONTENTS

Maps 3

List of Illustrations 4

Acknowledgments 5

Prologue 7

Chapter One - On The Warpath: 1780 17

Chapter Two - Van Etten's Command 25

Chapter Three - Klader's Detachment 31

Chapter Four - The Shadow of Death:
                September 11, 1780 37

Chapter Five - Balliet's Detail 45

Chapter Six - Frontier Endgame: 1781-1783 61

Chapter Seven - Turnips and Venison 69

Epilogue 73

Appendix A: Letter from Lieutenant Colonel Stephen Balliet
                   to Joseph Reed, Esquire of Philadelphia,
                   September 20, 1780 77

Appendix B: Captain Johannes Van Etten's Company of
                   Volunteers, Northampton County,
                   Pennsylvania, January 15, 1781 79

Appendix C: The Canandaigua Treaty of 1794 83

1

Notes 87

Bibliography 93

Index 99

MAPS

Figure 1 - Land of the Iroquois 16

Figure 2 - Key to the Indian Paths of Pennsylvania 23

Figure 3 - Old Indian Trails: The Nescopeck Path and
The Nanticoke Path 30

Figure 4 - Old Map of the Sugarloaf Massacre 35

Figure 5 - Sugarloaf Township, Pennsylvania 67

LIST OF ILLUSTRATIONS

The illustrations listed below appear as a group beginning on page 53.

1. The Sugarloaf Massacre Memorial, Sugarloaf, PA.

2. Bronze Plaque, Sugarloaf Massacre Memorial.

3. Gravestone of Captain Daniel Klader, near massacre site.

4. The Pine Grove. In the foreground, the "bloodstained field."

5. The white pine staff marks the spot where the old oak tree stood over Klader's grave.

6. Close-up of the spot where Klader is buried. His men lie nearby in a common grave.

7. The Little Nescopeck Creek at Conyngham, PA.

8. The Little Nescopeck Creek flows towards the "Big Nescopeck."

ACKNOWLEDGMENTS

This book would not have been possible without the assistance of many people. I am grateful to each for their kindness and professional courtesy.

A number of Pennsylvania libraries were of great utility. The staff of the Hazleton Public Library were helpful in granting the author access to their Pennsylvania Historical Collection. They were also able to secure a number of useful books through interlibrary loan. The staff of the Eastern Monroe County Public Library in Stroudsburg provided assistance. Lehigh Carbon Community College'e library in Schnecksville was also of great utility. The Osterhout Free Library in Wilkes-Barre was quite useful. The staffs at these libraries were both friendly and helpful.

The volunteers at the Monroe County Historical Society provided essential background into the Northampton County Militia during the American Revolution. The staff of the Wyoming Historical and Geological Society in Wilkes-Barre generously provided their expertise.

A number of Pennsylvanians rallied to the cause. Thomas Bainbridge of Conyngham provided an introduction to Attorney Paula DeJoseph. She graciously permitted the author access to the battlefield from her adjoining property. Joan Foose of Nuremberg shot the photographs that appear in this book. Her assistance is greatly appreciated. Anita Zius of Hazleton provided needed word processing skills and created a presentable finished product.

A number of individuals provided assistance at various points in the project. They include: Ruth Bowen, Bob Carberry, Rosanne Catalfomo, Jane Dougherty, Larry Kelly, Alexis Neapolitan, Jr., John Orlondini, James Reinmiller, Attorney James Schneider, Alan Smith and Dennis Ulrich. This book could not have been completed without them.

Rogan Hart Moore
June 25, 2000
Conyngham, Pennsylvania

5

On September 11, 1780, a detachment of forty-one Northampton County, Pennsylvania, militiamen was surprised by a force consisting of thirty Seneca warriors and Tories. When the fighting was over, fifteen American patriots lay dead on the ground. Three more were taken prisoner, the remainder scattered throughout what is today the Sugarloaf Valley of Northeastern Pennsylvania.

When juxtaposed with the major engagements of the American Revolution, the Sugarloaf Massacre can be viewed as a rather insignificant skirmish fought in the wilderness of Pennsylvania's Susquehanna frontier. For the combatants, however, this "mere skirmish" was a searing convulsion of hand-to-hand combat fought in the midday heat of late summer, in which Seneca tomahawks and patriot sidearms were utilized with savage ferocity. Throats were cut, skulls were smashed. Men were shot, tomahawked, tortured, scalped. When the frenzy of killing finally abated, the blood of patriot and Iroquois alike oozed into the rich soil that would someday be part of the Wagner Farm near Conyngham, Pennsylvania.

A memorial erected near the spot in 1933 by the Pennsylvania Historical Commission, the Wyoming Historical and Geological Society and the Sugarloaf Commemorative Committee, recorded that on September 11, 1780, a detachment of Captain John Van Etten's Company of Northampton County Militia resting at the spring (the Little Nescopeck Creek), was surprised by a band of Indians and Tories led by the Seneca Chief Roland Montour. Those who perished were Captain Daniel Klader, Corporal Samuel Bond and Privates Jacob Arndt, Peter Croom, Philip George, Abraham Klader, John Kouts, James McGraw, Paul Neely, George Peter Renhart, Jacob Row, George Shilhamer, Abraham Smith, Baltzer Snyder and John Weaver. Accounts of Seneca and Tory casualties vary. It is known that Roland Montour died a week after the fight from wounds suffered during the engagement.[1]

The story of the Sugarloaf Massacre has been passed down through the generations. Word of the tragedy was first reported by Lieutenant John Myer to the command at Fort Wyoming. Myer, who with two others was captured and taken prisoner by Montour, managed somehow to escape. He found his way to safety. Myer arrived exhausted and famished at Fort Wyoming on Thursday, September 14th. Six days later Lieutenant Colonel Stephen Balliet of the Northampton County Militia informed Joseph Reed, Esquire, President of the Supreme Executive Council of Pennsylvania, of the massacre and the subsequent expedition to recover and bury the dead of Klader's detachment.

Some survivors of the massacre lived until the middle of the nineteenth century. An oral tradition developed and embellished accounts of the combat were passed down through the generations in fireside stories. Some of these claim that Captain Klader was responsible for four, perhaps seven Iroquois deaths. A different tale claims that his brother Abraham survived the battle after submerging himself in the creek to avoid the enemy. Frederick Shickler is said to have fled over Buck Mountain leaving the Indian trail to his right while keeping out of sight of the advancing Senecas, yet this company had no man named Shickler on its muster rolls. One more tale tells of a hapless young patriot losing his life after his faithful dog's barking alerted the Senecas to his hiding place.

In September 1866, an account of the Sugarloaf Massacre written by journalist John C. Stokes, appeared in the "Hazleton Sentinel" newspaper. By the 1930s William Tilden Stauffer of the Sugarloaf Historical Association was writing more newspaper articles on the subject. Stauffer was instrumental in securing a permanent memorial on the site in 1933. In 1947, a State Historical Marker on the Sugarloaf Massacre was erected on Route 93, five miles northwest of Hazleton, near Conyngham, Pennsylvania. It records that "after an unsuccessful attack on Fort Augusta, Indians and Tories surprised a detachment of Northampton County Militia on September 11, 1780. The site of the massacre is just beyond the town."[2]

Brief accounts of the Sugarloaf Massacre have appeared in local and regional histories since the decade of the 1840s when William L. Stone and Charles Miner both wrote histories of the Wyoming Valley. Several brief renditions of the massacre appeared in later histories of Northeastern and East-Central Pennsylvania, but like their newspaper counterparts facts were scarce and often confused. A number of inconsistencies evident in extant accounts of the Sugarloaf Massacre have created obstacles to research. While many facts lie shrouded in obfuscation, a sufficiency remain, providing insight into the calamity along the Little Nescopeck Creek.

While the roots of the Sugarloaf Massacre can be traced to at least the seventeenth century, this work will focus on the often violent interaction between the Iroquois and white settlers in the raucous Susquehanna frontier of the American Revolution.

Bunker Hill, Washington's Crossing, Trenton, Valley Forge, Saratoga and Yorktown. These names come readily to mind when one considers the American Revolution. American mythology has transformed the Revolutionary War for many into a bloodless chess match played out by aristocratic gentlemen in powdered, white wigs. But the grim realities of the American Revolution were far deadlier. For Washington's army the Revolution was a bloody and desperate struggle to break the will of the British to wage war against them. The British, grimly determined to maintain their hegemony in the thirteen colonies, waged war with genuine intensity. An American defeat would certainly have cost any captured, self-styled patriots their lives, their fortunes and their sacred honor. While the names recalled above have earned a hallowed place in the annals of American history, the lesser known forests and valleys of the Iroquois witnessed some of the most savage fighting of the Revolutionary War.

The Susquehanna frontier of Northeastern Pennsylvania and the great expanse of territory in New York once controlled by the Six Nations of the Iroquois Confederacy was in the eighteenth century part of America's northwestern frontier. Like the "wild west" of the Great Plains a century later, the frontier settlements of Iroquoia brimmed with tales of ambushes, Indian raids, kidnappings and scalpings. The

American Revolution in the eighteenth century west became a confusing ferment of mixed loyalties and savagery on all sides which culminated with the use of biological warfare, terrorism and a campaign of ethnic cleansing.

The Sullivan Expedition against the Six Nations in the summer and early autumn of 1779 was a defining event in American history. The campaign marked the inception of a concerted effort on the part of the United States to subdue the Native American population. The subjugation of the Iroquois began a terrible process that would come to include such bitter tragedies as the "trail of tears," and the infamous massacre of the Sioux at Wounded Knee, South Dakota, in 1890. The achievement of "Manifest Destiny" came at an enormous price.

The plan to quell the threat posed to the frontier settlements in New York and Pennsylvania was conceived by George Washington himself. Born at Valley Forge in the fifth year of the American Revolution, Washington's plan sought to negate the Tory-Iroquois alliance that had wreaked havoc on settlers at New York's Cherry Valley in 1777 and in the Wyoming Valley of Northeastern Pennsylvania the following year. The execution of this plan in the field would ultimately fall to Major General John Sullivan of New Hampshire.

Sullivan's army marched from the banks of the Delaware River at Easton, north through the Pocono Mountains to the Wyoming Valley and the banks of the Susquehanna River. From there they pushed further north into the heart of Iroquois territory around the Finger Lakes, ultimately pressing west to the Genesee River. The arduous trek homewards came next. The expedition severely tested the logistical capabilities of this eighteenth century army. In command of four brigades of Continentals, Sullivan faced a population of approximately fifteen thousand Iroquois and an essentially indeterminate number of Tory militia. Largely due to the diplomatic efforts of the Reverend Samuel Kirkland who accompanied the expedition, not all of the Indians proved hostile. Sullivan's command laid waste to forty Iroquois settlements and destroyed 160,000 acres of corn. For this the Iroquois dubbed Sullivan "The Corn Cutter." Washington became known as "The Town Destroyer."[3]

The army ravaged the Iroquois homeland, but the stated goal of pacifying the Susquehanna frontier was never fully achieved. The Iroquois spent the remainder of the war years seeking vengeance for Sullivan's incursion into their territory. In Northeastern Pennsylvania, the warlike Seneca chieftain Roland Montour proved himself an intractable foe of further white settlement. While Washington was achieving greater fame as the Commander-in-Chief of the Continental Army, Sullivan tendered the resignation of his commission to the Continental Congress and returned home to his native New Hampshire embittered and exhausted.

The campaign against the Iroquois posed a profound conundrum for John Sullivan. Born in New Hampshire of Irish parentage, he was innately sensitive to the plight of oppressed peoples. Having grown up on stories of British injustice in Ireland, he rushed to the patriot cause and made a name for himself early in the American Revolution. His ancestors had found themselves fighting fellow Irishmen in the political upheavals of seventeenth century Ireland and had suffered under the Penal Laws. Some empathy towards the Iroquois, the people he was ordered to wage war upon, was perhaps inevitable. While this empathy in no way interfered with Sullivan's ability to command, it combined with his dissatisfaction over the perceived inadequate supply of his army to darken his moods. Sullivan also resented those in command positions he felt were determined to undermine him. His recusing attitude managed to antagonize many who might otherwise have been useful to his endeavors.

Sullivan's foes, the Six Nations of the Iroquois Confederacy, had once been known as the Five Nations. By 1723, they had accepted the Iroquoian speaking Tuscarora tribe into their Confederacy. The Mohawks were the easternmost of the six tribes and lived to the south of the Mohawk River. Beyond them to the west were the Oneidas. They lived by the shores of Oneida Lake. The Onondagas were to the west of the Oneida tribe, residing along the Onondaga River. The Cayuga tribe lived along Cayuga Lake, while the Senecas occupied land along the Genesee River. A robust and warlike people with a highly developed social structure that has at times been described as something of a primitive democracy, the Iroquois were themselves a complex dichotomy.[4]

The British, for their part, never committed a great number of regular troops to the northwestern theatre of operations after General Burgoyne's defeat at Saratoga in 1777. Preferring to rely on the efforts of loyalist militia, notably an impressive unit known as "Butler's Rangers," along with their allies amongst the Iroquois, they contented themselves for the duration of the war with harassing frontier raids.

With his headquarters at Fort Niagara, Colonel Guy Johnson succeeded his father-in-law as Superintendent of Indian Affairs for the British Crown. Serving in this post from 1774 until 1782, Johnson was able to maintain the loyalty of most of the Iroquois throughout the American Revolution. If Washington had a nemesis on the northwestern frontier during these turbulent years, then surely it was Guy Johnson. It fell to Major General John Sullivan to serve as the instrument of Washington's retribution upon Johnson and his allies.

The Sullivan Expedition's place in American history was virtually ignored by nationalist school historians in the nineteenth century. Local historians in New York and Pennsylvania attempted to elevate the importance of the campaign. In 1868, Thomas C. Amory wrote *The Military Services and Public Life of Major-General John Sullivan, of the Revolutionary Army*. It stood as the only biography of the General for nearly a century. In 1961, Charles P. Whittemore's work, *A General of the Revolution: John Sullivan of New Hampshire*, was published. Despite these books, accounts of Sullivan's Expedition remained fragmentary until recent times. Whittemore's biography, emerging out of his doctoral dissertation at Columbia, opened the door to further inquiry into the life and times of an American enigma.

In the past decade at least three books have been published on Sullivan. *Painted in Blood: Remember Wyoming! America's First Civil War*, by Jay L. Glickman, was published in 1997. In this book the author reasserted the expansive view of nineteenth century local historians from New York and Pennsylvania while presenting a riveting account of the Wyoming Massacre of 1778. Also published in 1997, Joseph R. Fischer's book entitled *A Well-Executed Failure: The Sullivan Campaign Against the Iroquois, July-September 1779,* presented a brilliant account of the Sullivan Expedition. The author appraised virtually the totality of the military operation. Fischer's thesis that the Sullivan Campaign was a well-executed failure is indeed compelling.[5] Max M. Mintz wrote *Seeds of Empire: The American Revolutionary Conquest of the Iroquois.* Published in 1999, this book exemplifies the author's many years of scholarship in this area.

Barbara Graymont of Syracuse University has been a steadfast champion of the rights of the Iroquois. Her assertion that the Sullivan Expedition drove the Iroquois to acts of greater desperation which were manifest in the frontier violence of 1780 is also compelling.[6] Recently published books and numerous published articles of contemporary vintage have combined with earlier scholarship to demonstrate the continued interest in this chapter of American history. The Sullivan Expedition against the Iroquois continues to both fascinate and perplex.

The military engagement known as the Sugarloaf Massacre occurred a year after Sullivan's Expedition supposedly pacified the hostile Iroquois of the northwestern frontier, and more than two years after the Wyoming Massacre had taken place in the Wyoming Valley. Clashes with the Iroquois would occur until the end of the Revolutionary War. The Iroquois Confederacy, weakened and divided by mixed loyalties during the war, would ultimately be shattered after it. White settlers would stream into lands that had once been part of Iroquoia after the American Revolution. The Sugarloaf Valley would be settled in the years immediately following the war by Pennsylvania Germans. An ironic twist of fate. Captain Klader's ill-fated detachment had consisted mostly of these Pennsylvania "Dutchmen."

The Sugarloaf Valley is an area known not only for its scenic beauty, but also for its rich history. Native Americans utilized the valley for centuries to hunt and fish. They followed predictable trails through a rugged area that both the Delaware and Iroquois regarded as part of a great wilderness. Two Indian trails passed through the Sugarloaf Valley.

The Nescopeck Trail joined the forks of the Delaware River near Easton with the Delaware Indian settlement near Nescopeck, Pennsylvania. It crossed the Sugarloaf Valley approximately one-quarter mile east of what is today Main Street in Conyngham. The Nescopeck Path was one of the main escape routes for the victims of the Wyoming Massacre of 1778. The path was generally only eighteen inches in width and grew to be a foot in depth due to heavy usage. It passed through the Sugarloaf Valley on its way to the Lehigh River and on to Fort Allen near Weissport. Fort Allen was one of a series of frontier forts built along the ridge of Blue Mountain designed to protect the more settled region of Southeastern Pennsylvania from Indian incursions.

A second path, known as the Nanticoke Trail, also passed through the Sugarloaf Valley and stretched from near Binghampton, New York, south to the Chesapeake Bay.

The most impressive geological feature in the Sugarloaf Valley is surely the Sugarloaf Mountain. This beautiful, conical protuberance was so named because it was thought to resemble a lump of sugar. In 1787, an early surveyor noted a "Sugarloaf Hill" on a map he was drawing in a survey for a landowner named William Gray. The mountain rests impressively in a scenic valley bordered to the east by the Buck Mountain and to the west by the Nescopeck Mountain. Beyond the Buck Mountain was a soggy patch of ground known to the Pennsylvania Dutch as the "Haselschwamp."[7] Beyond the Nescopeck Mountain was the village of Nescopeck and the Susquehanna River itself.

The Nescopeck Creek, a tributary of the Susquehanna River, cuts through the Sugarloaf Valley. The Little Nescopeck Creek is a tributary of the Nescopeck and peters out into a number of small streams in the valley. The Sugarloaf Massacre did not occur on the Sugarloaf Mountain as many have erroneously believed. It was by the Little Nescopeck Creek, not far from the Nescopeck and Buck

Mountain that Captain Klader's detachment was surprised by a force of Iroquois and Tories that summer day in 1780. Time has not been kind to the old battlefield. The Senecas carried away their wounded and dead, but the scalped, mutilated, naked bodies of the fallen patriots lay prostrate on the ground for more than six days before a hastily assembled burial detail could place them in a mass grave. Like so many other battlefields, the bloodstained field by the Little Nescopeck has become virtually imperceptible. Beneath the rich soil of Sugarloaf fifteen American patriots who made the ultimate sacrifice sleep for eternity.

Figure 1 (Map)   Land of the Iroquois

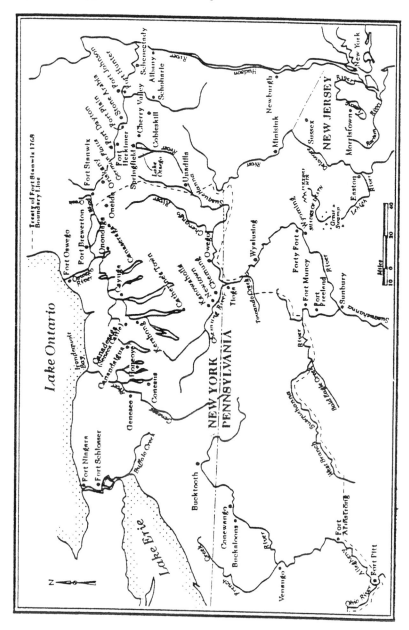

Chapter One

ON THE WARPATH: 1780

Sullivan's Expedition against the Iroquois in 1779 failed to pacify the frontier. No sooner had his army withdrawn from Iroquoia than the Indians began planning a campaign of retribution. Their lands laid waste by Sullivan's retiring army, their homes destroyed, the Iroquois approached the winter of 1779-1780 with trepidation. That winter was most severe. For weeks snow drifts several feet high covered the barren ground. Temperatures persisted well below freezing. Wildlife perished in the fields and forests of New York and Pennsylvania. Hunters searched for game to no avail. Hundreds of Iroquois froze or starved to death during that dreadful season. Misery abounded.

In February of 1780, the Iroquois began forming war parties for the coming campaign. The Cayuga chieftain Hojiagede told Colonel Guy Johnson at Fort Niagara that he had recruited nearly ninety braves ready for the fight. The legendary Mohawk chieftain Thayendanegea, known to whites as Joseph Brant, conducted a ritual war dance at the home of Colonel Johnson on the 7th of February. Three days later the Nanticoke Captain Shinop met with Johnson and told him that his war party consisting of twenty-one warriors would set out in a few days. He expected to supplement his force with some Shawnee braves. On February 11, two hundred thirty Indians and six Tories departed Fort Niagara for the wilderness of New York. This force consisted mostly of Cayugas, Tuteloes, Mohawks, Onondagas, Senecas and Delawares.

After Brant's departure several other war parties joined him in the field. On the 16th Captain Shinop set out with some twenty-five warriors. He headed for the Susquehanna frontier and the Wyoming Valley of Northeastern Pennsylvania. Indians returning to Fort Niagara from various hunting expeditions saw the departing warriors and joined them in significant numbers. On the 26th another war party, this one led by Chief Little Beard and Tanaghkewas with sixteen braves left the fort. About that time the Seneca chieftain Roland

Montour with eight warriors and Chief Fish Hook with another fifteen also departed on the warpath.[1]

By July 1, nearly five hundred Indians and Tories had entered the field determined to avenge their losses of the previous year. For about eight months several hundred of these warriors raged across the northwestern frontier inflicting great losses in both American blood and treasure.

On March 21, the garrison at Shenesboro, New York, was defeated. The small force of thirteen militiamen was captured. On April 7, another fourteen prisoners were added to this number after a scouting party commanded by Captain Alexander Harper was overpowered. More Americans were taken captive later. Rather than risk an assault on Fort Schoharie, Brant decided to return to Fort Niagara and unburden his force of its prisoners.

Captives who could not keep up with an Iroquois war party were often killed. The wounded generally suffered a similar fate. Hiakatoo, the husband of Mary Jemison, gave no quarter while on the warpath. Jemison would later relate the cruelties inflicted upon the enemies of the Iroquois, which included beating the brains out of infants, mutilation, scalping and torturing. Defiling the bodies of the slain and torturing captives were both of religious significance to the Iroquois. Scalps were deemed to be sacred objects, even a fair substitute for a relative killed in battle. But the Iroquois were not the only warriors to fight with savage intensity. Americans also took scalps and frequently mistreated prisoners. Bounties were paid for scalps by both sides. Indeed, Pennsylvania had offered bounties for Indian scalps as early as the French and Indian War. The practice was resumed during the Indian wars of the 1760s. British General Henry Hamilton, known as "Hair Buyer," offered the equivalent of $50.00 for each American scalp received.[2]

An Iroquois war party entered the Wyoming Valley of Northeastern Pennsylvania on March 27. Thomas Bennet of Kingston and his son were captured. Another Wyoming Valley resident, Lebbeus Hammond, had been captured a few hours earlier. Hammond, a survivor of the Wyoming Massacre of 1778, began to look for a means of escape. Managing to get hold of a spear carelessly left by an Indian guard while the rest of the war party slept, Bennet cut through his ropes and freed himself. He quickly thrust the spear through the side of the hapless Indian who fell dead into the fire. Hammond and the younger Bennet were cut loose. Three members of the war party were tomahawked in their sleep, a fourth badly wounded. The three fortunate frontiersmen arrived at the relative safety of Fort Wyoming on the evening of the 30th.

Another war party, a band of ten Indians, shot Asa Upson near Hanover, Pennsylvania, on the same day that Hammond and the two Bennets were abducted. Similar incidents occurred throughout the Wyoming Valley. A Wilkes-Barre man was killed while making sugar on the 28th near his home. Another was wounded. Then a youth named Jonah Rogers was captured by the Iroquois in the lower part of the valley.

The Moses Van Campen family was taken prisoner on the 30th. At least three men in that family were killed and scalped. Others were captured. Skirmishes flared up throughout the Wyoming Valley between contingents of Captain John Franklin's militia and marauding bands of Iroquois and Tories. Abraham Pike and his family were captured soon after the incident with the Van Campens.

On the night of April 3, Moses Van Campen initiated a miraculous escape from his sleeping captors. Managing to secure a knife he cut himself loose and then freed the others. Muskets were silently removed and then the Indians were tomahawked as they slept. A brief scuffle ensued, but Van Campen's party made quick work of it. After scalping the dead Indians, and gathering up the scalps of the American dead, Van Campen's party escaped. A raft was hastily built on the shores of the Susquehanna River. They arrived at Fort Wyoming, like the Bennet and Hammond party before them, with a harrowing tale to tell.[3]

Joseph Reed wrote to Colonel Samuel Hunter on April 7 authorizing him "to offer the following premiums for every male prisoner whether white or Indian, if the former is acting with the latter, fifteen hundred dollars, and one thousand dollars for every Indian scalp." Four days later Reed wrote to Colonel Jacob Stroud, "We have therefore authorized Lieutenant of the county (Northampton) to offer fifteen hundred dollars for every Indian or Tory prisoner taken in arms against us, and one thousand dollars for every Indian scalp."[4] Despite some initial reluctance, scalping parties were soon operative. At one point some thirteen scalps were sent in a package to Fort Pitt for payment. The Pennsylvania bounty law fell into disrepute as friendly Indians were at times killed for their scalps. Payment for scalps continued until the autumn of 1782 when General Sir Guy Carleton effectively ended Britain's alliance with the Iroquois.

On April 25, the Benjamin Gilbert family, living near the Mahoning Creek in what is today Carbon County, Pennsylvania, was captured by a war party of eleven Indians. Ironically, the Gilberts lived a mere five or six miles from Fort Allen, one of the frontier forts along the Blue Mountain designed to protect the region from hostiles. The family was Quaker and had relocated from Byberry, near Philadelphia, in 1775. They farmed, built a log cabin, a barn, and then a saw and grist mill. For five years they resided in this location, typical frontier settlers of the day. Taken captive that day were Benjamin Gilbert, Sr., his wife Elizabeth, sons Joseph, Jesse, and Abner Gilbert, daughters Rebecca and Elizabeth. Jesse's wife Sarah Gilbert, Thomas Peart, Benjamin Gilbert, son of John Gilbert of Philadelphia, Andrew Harrigar, a hireling, and Abigail Dodson, the daughter of Samuel Dodson, were also taken. With twelve captives the Indians moved to the nearby home of Benjamin Peart. They seized Benjamin, his wife Elizabeth, and their infant child, just nine months old. Now with fifteen prisoners the war party headed north, moving towards Fort Niagara. They walked over the Mauch Chunk and Broad Mountains of Northeastern Pennsylvania, then used the Nescopeck Trail, crossed the Quakake Creek and the Moravian Pine Swamp to Mahoning Mountain, where they camped that night.

The Iroquois secured their prisoners by cutting down a sapling as large as a man's thigh, cut notches in which they fixed their legs and then placed a pole, crossing it with stakes driven firmly into the ground. At the crotches of the stakes they added other poles which were placed on the backs of the prisoners, effectively restraining them. Straps were then put around the necks of the prisoners. These could be fastened to a tree. The Gilbert and Peart families spent their first night of captivity in this manner. Beds made up of hemlock branches strewn on the ground and blankets were provided, but it was a terrifying experience for the captives nonetheless.

On the 26th they were dragged on towards the Susquehanna River. Benjamin Gilbert, Sr., began to falter. He had already been marked for death with black face paint by the Indians and now found himself with a rope around his neck. His end was nigh. Suddenly his wife Elizabeth began to plead for his life. The Indians relented. Somehow the two families made their way into Canada without any loss of life. Benjamin Gilbert, Sr., would tell Chief Montour that, "He had brought in the oldest man and the youngest child." Montour replied that, "It was not I, but the great God, who brought you through, for we were determined to kill you, but were prevented."[5]

On June 17, the two families endured the ordeal of the gauntlet. Finally released from their restraints, they faced a throng of Indians bearing clubs and stones. They were mercilessly beaten. Blood gushed from their heads. Bones were broken and crushed. With their closely cropped and matted hair, filthy rags and grotesque wounds, they made a pitiful spectacle. Their lives were spared by an Iroquois chief who declared that they had suffered sufficiently. Forcibly separated from one another, some were adopted by the Iroquois, others sent down Lake Ontario to Montreal. It was all too much for old Benjamin Gilbert. Already broken in body and spirit, he died under the strain that summer. Gilbert was buried under an oak tree near the fort of Coeur du Lac, on the St. Lawrence River, below Ogdensburg. The remainder of the Gilbert and Peart families would remain captives in Iroquoia until August 22, 1782, when they were collected at Montreal and eventually returned to Byberry, Pennsylvania.

By May 21, 1780 Sir John Johnson had moved south from Canada into Tryon County, New York, destroying American settlements on the north side of the Mohawk River. Nine New Yorkers were killed and thirty-three taken prisoner. The Iroquois rampaged throughout the surrounding countryside. Colonel John Harper at the head of about three hundred militia trailed the attackers to Johnstown, New York, but judging them too strong a force, chose not to instigate a major engagement.

While Johnson's strike force retired in good order, pressure was placed upon the Oneidas and Tuscaroras to join the pro-British alliance. Fearing retribution, the Oneidas sought the protection of the Fort Stanwix garrison. They were too late. War parties began to form in the Oneida territory. On June 24 the Mohawk David Hill and Captain John McDonnell of Butler's Rangers began to threaten and cajole the Oneidas into an alliance. By July 2 about three hundred Oneidas, Tuscaroras and reluctant Onondagas agreed to serve the king.

Joseph Brant left Fort Niagara on July 11, with three hundred Indian warriors and more than a dozen Tories. His objective was the destruction of the remaining pro-American tribes in Iroquoia. By the end of that month Brant's force had burned the remaining Oneida and Tuscarora villages, plundered and killed their livestock and fired the church where the Reverend Samuel Kirkland had once preached. In early August the Canajoharie District was burned. Dozens of buildings were torched. Over four hundred Indians participated in this action. On August 9 Brant and a smaller war party attacked part of the Schoharie settlement. Eleven members of the Vrooman family were captured and three killed. The three dead included the Vrooman parents and an eight year old boy named Peter. He was viciously killed by a Tory named Benjamin Beacraft who slit his throat from ear to ear and then scalped him.[6]

By mid-summer New York and the northern tier of Pennsylvania were in the midst of a military crisis. A series of punitive raids from the Iroquois and Butler's Rangers had set the frontier aflame. The stage was set for the bloody skirmish on the Little Nescopeck Creek known as the Sugarloaf Massacre.

Figure 2 (Map) -   Key to the Indian Paths of Pennsylvania

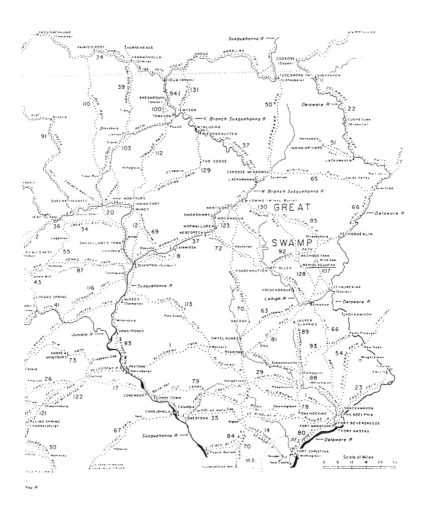

Chapter Two

VAN ETTEN'S COMMAND

As Iroquois war parties and contingents of loyalist troops ravaged the frontier, patriot militias were hastily assembled and mustered into active service. A company of volunteers was formed in Northampton County, Pennsylvania, on June 15, 1780. They were to serve for a period of seven months. Commanded by Captain Johannes Van Etten, a veteran of the French and Indian War, this company began to drill at Fort Penn. The fort had been built by Colonel Jacob Stroud and had served as a refuge from attack following the Battle of Wyoming of July 3, 1778. Named in honor of Governor John Penn, Fort Penn replaced Fort Hamilton which stood nearby. The latter had been built in 1756 under the direction of Benjamin Franklin.

Jacob Stroud served as a member of the Pennsylvania State Constitutional Convention in 1776, in the state legislature, 1781-1783, then founded Stroudsburg in 1799. A wooden stockade once surrounded the Stroud home which served as the nucleus of the fort. Today the Stroud "mansion" houses the Monroe County Historical Society.

Captain Van Etten, the son of Jacob Van Etten and the former Antje Westbrook, was one of five children. Born in New Jersey around 1730 and raised in the Delaware Valley, he served with distinction during the French and Indian War. Van Etten kept a wartime journal in 1756 and 1757. He commanded at various times, both Fort Hamilton and Fort Hyndshaw. These forts were situated in the Pocono Mountains of Northeastern Pennsylvania, part of an extended chain of forts stretching west along the Blue Mountain to Fort Augusta.

Benjamin Franklin wrote to Captain Van Etten on January 12, 1756, instructing him to raise a company of thirty men and to keep a daily journal. Franklin wrote that "you are to take care that the men keep their arms clean and in good order and that their powder be always kept dry and fit for use."[1][2]

Van Etten became one of the justices of Northampton County, Pennsylvania. On March 21, 1756 he wrote in his journal, "I went on my journey to Easton in order to attend Court, leaving the charge of the company to the lieutenant. Being obliged to tarry by reason of the weather, I attended the whole term." A week later he "returned home safe to the fort finding my men in health and all things in good order." The next day he drilled the men and hauled firewood.[2]

Captain Van Etten's sword and his New Testament became treasures passed down through the generations in his family. His saddle bags were also saved. In 1925, his descendant Lila Van Etten Huddy wrote that "the Testament had become curved from the saddle bags strapped around the horse in its use during the war."[3]

Johannes Van Etten married Maria Gonzales at Napanoch, New York, in 1750. He settled in Pennsylvania, served effectively in the French and Indian War and again during the American Revolution. Johannes and Maria had at least nine children, perhaps eleven. These included Johannes, Jr., Magdalena, Manuel, Rymerick, Elizabeth, James, Anthony, Catherine and Simeon. After Maria Gonzales Van Etten died the Captain took Rachael Williams as his second wife. She was the widow of Daniel Decker of Northampton County. Johannes and Rachael Van Etten had four children: Daniel, Cornelius, Solomon and Dorothy.

By the time that Van Etten was assigned to command a Company of Northampton County Volunteers in 1780 he was already a man of about fifty. The descendant of a long line of Dutchmen originally from the town of Etten in the Netherlands, Van Etten found himself commanding a company consisting mostly of "Pennsylvania Dutchmen." This company was activated on June 15, 1780 and served until January 15, 1781, a period of seven months. Van Etten's command began their active service at Fort Penn and while some ended it there seven months later, fifteen were killed in action on September 11. Military service after the Sugarloaf Massacre proved too much for

Private Philip Bitten. He deserted Van Etten's Company on November 10.[4]

Corporal Adam Hecker enlisted in Van Etten's Company on July 11, 1780. He was born in 1756, the son of the Reverend John Egidius Hecker, a minister of the Reformed Church, and died in 1815. Adam Hecker married Susanna Engel and fathered eight children. The Reverend Hecker was pastor of the Springfield Reformed Congregation in Bucks County and another congregation in Moore Township, Northampton County, where he lies buried. Reverend Hecker graduated in 1750 from the University of Herborn and came to America in 1751. Born in 1726 at Dillenberg, he was the son of John Wigand Hecker, equerry to Prince Christian, the last of the Nassau Dillenberg princes. The Hecker family had lived in the area of Dillenberg for generations. Corporal Hecker's grandfather was Frederick Christian Hecker.

Private Rudolph Smith enlisted on June 17, 1780. He was the son of Rudolph Smith of Salisbury Township, now part of Lehigh County. His brother was Private Daniel Smith of the same company.

Private George Gangawere enlisted on June 17, 1780. He was born in 1756 and had prior military service. Gangawere was a fifter from January 13, 1776 in Captain Thomas Craig's Company of Colonel St. Clair's Second Pennsylvania Battalion and served in Canada. He was mustered out on November 25, 1776 and later served with two other companies. He lived in Whitehall Township, Northampton County, where he kept a tavern after the war.

George Gangawere married Christiana Klader, the daughter of Valentine Klader. Christiana's brother, Captain Daniel Klader, would lead a detachment of Van Etten's command into what was then called the "Scotch Valley" in September 1780. Private George Gangawere was Captain Klader's brother-in-law. Gangawere died in 1852 at the age of 95. He was probably the grandson of Jacob Gangawere who came to America in 1727. The family was known for its longevity.

Private Philip George Shellhammer who enlisted on August 7, 1780 was likely Philip Jacob Shellhammer, born in 1759, died 1836, of Penn Township, Northampton County, now East Penn Township, Schuylkill County. Private George Shellhammer who enlisted on August 17, 1780, and was killed at the Sugarloaf Massacre, was of the same family.[5]

Private Paul Neely enlisted on July 18, 1780 and was also killed on September 11. He was probably Paul Neligh, the son of Henry Neligh, of Whitehall Township, who died in 1774.

Private John Knapsnyder was a resident of Moore Township Northampton County and Private Samuel Summeny, who enlisted on July 25, 1780, lived in Towamensing Township also in Northampton County.

Private Adam Brunthaver enlisted on June 15, 1780. He was born on December 21, 1748 in the Alsace. Brunthaver came to America prior to the Revolution and settled in Moore Township, Northampton County, where he was a farmer and a tailor. In 1775 he traveled to Allentown and left for the war with six to eight men, one of whom was Philip Deily of Heidelberg Township. After a brief sojourn in Easton they traveled under the command of Lieutenant Kern, arriving in Boston a few days prior to the Battle of Bunker Hill. In 1776 Brunthaver enlisted in Captain Thomas Craig's Company, reenlisted in 1777 and served again later in the war. After the American Revolution, Brunthaver moved west and settled in Westmoreland County, Pennsylvania. He died there on July 29, 1834.

Captain Daniel Klader's family had originated in Switzerland and migrated to the German Palatine prior to coming to America. His father, Valentine, was born in the Palatine on June 17, 1726. He arrived in Philadelphia on September 20, 1743, an aspiring pioneer of seventeen. Valentine Klader became a carpenter and pursued his trade along the Monocacy Creek near Bethlehem. The elder Klader cleared the ground, tilled the soil, and built a cabin. He returned to the Palatine in 1748 and married Anna Catherine Busz. The couple resided in Bethlehem Township until Valentine's death on August 7,

1775. Klader died the father of nine children, six girls and three boys. All three boys would serve the cause of liberty during the American Revolution.

Jacob Klader, the eldest of the three brothers, enlisted as a Private on March 1, 1776 and served in New York and Canada. After his honorable discharge from the Pennsylvania Continental Line he became a Captain of Northampton County Militia and saw active service in the field in November 1781 and again in May 1782. Jacob Klader ended his days as a popular tavern keeper and wealthy land owner in the Lehigh Valley. Jacob's brother Daniel Klader, had distinguished himself in the Pennsylvania Continental Line under General Anthony Wayne and later became a Captain of Northampton County Militia. He would die with his younger brother Abraham, a militia Private, during the Sugarloaf Massacre.

The large numbers of Pennsylvania Germans serving in Van Etten's Company of Volunteers was not unusual. Thousands of Pennsylvania Germans either served in the regular troops or militia, while others ground grain and furnished wood for the army, collected blankets for the soldiers, made guns, manufactured leather saddles and scabbards, cobbled shoes and tended to the sick and wounded. After the war most returned to the family farm.

As the summer of 1780 began to wane, a detachment of forty-one of the veteran Van Etten's Company was assigned to an imposing twenty-five year old Captain named Daniel Klader. Klader would lead these men into hostile and physically demanding terrain on a mission that culminated in tragedy.

Figure 3 (Map)   Old Indian Trails:
                             The Nescopeck Path and the Nanticoke Path

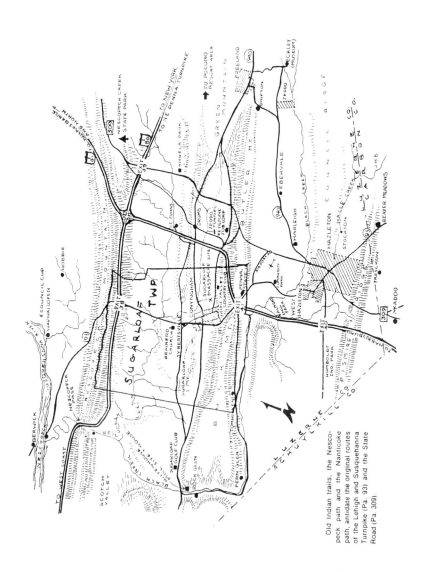

Old Indian trails, the Nescopeck path and the Nanticoke
path, antidate the original routes
of the Lehigh and Susquehanna
Turnpike (Pa. 93) and the State
Road (Pa. 309).

Chapter Three

KLADER'S DETACHMENT

Colonel Stephen Hunter, the Commanding Officer of Fort Augusta, ordered Captain Daniel Klader to take command of a detachment of Van Etten's Volunteer Militia. Klader was directed to select the best of Van Etten's Company for a dangerous mission that would take them into hostile country in search of Tory spies and sympathizers.[1] Klader would depart from Fort Penn and proceed to the banks of the Lehigh River at Fort Allen. From there he would move into the Sugarloaf Valley (then known as the "Scotch Valley"), where many loyalists were thought to reside. Klader would then join forces with other patriot troops at Fort Wyoming.

Captain Klader was at twenty-five, a powerful physical specimen, with a fine record of military service behind him. Hunter selected him for this assignment, passing over the experienced Van Etten. The veteran of the French and Indian War was now fifty, and considered to be past his fighting prime. This mission was a young man's duty. Klader and his men were chosen accordingly.

In early September, Captain Klader with forty Northampton County militiamen under his command, began the march from Fort Penn to Fort Allen. Among his men were his brother, Private Abraham Klader, and his brother-in-law Private George Gangawere. They marched from the Pocono Mountains through the Lehigh Valley to the Moravian settlement at Gnadenhuetten, where Weissport now stands. The fort, near the Lehigh River and the Blue Mountain, had featured prominently in the French and Indian War. After the Gilbert family was captured by an Iroquois war party, the fort was reinforced. Lieutenant Colonel Kern and one hundred twelve men were stationed at the fort as late as June 1, 1780. Fifteen miles to the east of the fort stood Fort Norris. As Klader's detachment approached Fort Allen, yet another frontier fort was coming under attack from the British and Iroquois.

31

On September 6, Fort Rice, near the Susquehanna River at Milton, Pennsylvania, was attacked by hundreds of Indians and Tories. The previous year, Fort Freeland had been sacked and burned. Captain John McDonald and a contingent of Seneca warriors led by Chief Hiakatoo, completely destroyed Fort Freeland. When Fort Freeland was attacked, John Montgomery sent two of his sons on horseback to a hill overlooking the scene. They were shocked at the ghastly sight of the fort going up in flames. The Montgomery family quickly abandoned their cabin and made for the Chillisquaque Creek and the cabin of Philip Davis. The Davis and Montgomery families reached safety at Fort Augusta. Montgomery's home was then burned by rampaging Senecas.

A new fort was erected to replace Fort Freeland. Built during the winter of 1779-1780, Fort Rice was a stockade with ready access to fresh water. The fort, consisting largely of limestone, was built by Captain John Rice and a detachment of Pennsylvania German troops. Because of its association with the Montgomery family, the fort has also been called "Fort Montgomery."

The British and Iroquois began their assault on Fort Rice around sundown on September 6. The garrison returned fire and after several volleys, managed to drive the enemy away. That night numerous fires could be seen by the hapless garrison defending the fort. Local homes, stacks of grain, and other buildings were destroyed by the marauders.[2]

A relief column of one hundred men under the command of Colonel John Kelly arrived from Fort Augusta the next day. Desperately in need of further reinforcements, Kelly sent a courier back to Colonel Hunter with an urgent request for more men. Hunter secured the services of Colonel Purdy who was marching towards Cumberland County with a body of militia. Purdy arrived at Fort Rice on September 9. A detachment from the fort went out in pursuit of the enemy and remained in the field until September 17. They returned to the fort in frustration. Their quarry had eluded them.

On Friday, September 8, two days after the attack on Fort Rice, Captain Klader's detachment departed Fort Allen. Forty-one men would make the laborious three-day trek to the Sugarloaf Valley. After a contentious fording of the Lehigh River near Gnadenheutten, Klader led his men west for about three miles through thick brush. He turned north through a gap in the hills and climbed Mauch Chunk Ridge near present-day Jim Thorpe. After a short rest, Klader's expedition proceeded along an old Indian trail known as the Lehigh Path. After reaching the top of Mauch Chunk Ridge, they followed the Nescopeck Path, crossed Mauch Chunk Creek, and climbed the Pisgah Mountain. Klader's men came down to greet the Nesquehoning Creek, fording it about one-half mile from its mouth. The Broad Mountain towered over them. It would wait until morning. The men made camp near the Nesquehoning Creek.

The Lehigh Path linked the forks of the Delaware River and the Lehigh Valley by way of Fort Allen to the Wyoming Valley of Northeastern Pennsylvania. It was terribly difficult terrain, mountainous, interspersed with areas of swamp land and swift flowing creeks. In 1779, Sullivan had chosen to take his army through the Wind Gap, a more meandering but less punishing course, better suited for his wagons and artillery. Klader chose to take the Lehigh Path to where it joined the Nescopeck Path as his detachment was on foot. The terrain was drier, the route more direct. Isaac Zane, who passed that way in 1758, was impressed with the "great hills and dales," the forests of straight white pine.[3] Not only was the terrain itself quite treacherous, but the wildlife native to the region could also intimidate. Black bear roamed the forests and swamps. Nights were shared with biting insects. Bobcats could spring from rocky crags. Copperheads and timber rattlesnakes were among the poisonous reptiles.

After the attack on Fort Rice the enemy broke into smaller war parties consisting of thirty to forty men. On September 9, a war party of forty Senecas and some Rangers under the command of Roland Montour and Lieutenant William Johnston marched against Fort Jenkins. Situated near the Susquehanna River about six and one-half miles northeast of Bloomsburg, the fort was a stockaded house. Montour and Johnston found the fort abandoned and expeditiously set it afire. After destroying the fort they ravaged the surrounding countryside. Cattle were rounded up, some prisoners taken. Ten men were detached from this war party to convey these prizes of war north to Fort Niagara. Montour was now in command of thirty warriors, all but a few of them Senecas.[4]

Captain Klader awoke his men that morning and began the punishing assault of the Broad Mountain. While Montour was destroying Fort Jenkins, Klader's men toiled over this steep spur overlooking the Lehigh River. The ascent was brutal indeed, but the men were up to the challenge. Descending the mountain, they reached the Quakake Creek later that day, and refreshed themselves in the cool water. After a brief respite, Klader drove his men over the Spring Mountain before encamping near the Beaver Creek. Before them lay a great expanse of wilderness known as the "Haselschwamp."

On Sunday, September 10, Captain Klader kept his men busy cleaning their rifles, fishing, foraging for wild game. He may have held a brief religious observance. There were probably conferences with his two subordinate officers, Lieutenant John Myer and Ensign James Scoby. On September 1, Scoby had been promoted to Ensign from the rank of Sergeant. Scouting parties may have roamed the local countryside. Sentries stood guard. The day appears to have passed relatively uneventfully.

From Klader's camp near the Beaver Creek, the Nescopeck Path progressed through the Hazle Swamp, part of the so-called "Great Swamp" enveloping much of Northeastern Pennsylvania.

Lieutenant Henry Dearborn, an officer under the command of General John Sullivan in 1779 described the thickest and most inhospitable section of this wilderness as "horrid, rough, gloomy country." Dearborn later served as Secretary of War under Thomas Jefferson. He called the densest part of the Great Swamp, the "Shades of Death." The Shades of Death had been aptly named.[5] In 1778, hundreds of refugees from the Wyoming Massacre fled through this wasteland on their way to Easton. Many died along the way. On September 11, 1780, the Sugarloaf Valley became a "valley of the shadow of death" for Captain Klader and his men.

Figure 4 (Map)   Old Map of the Sugarloaf Massacre

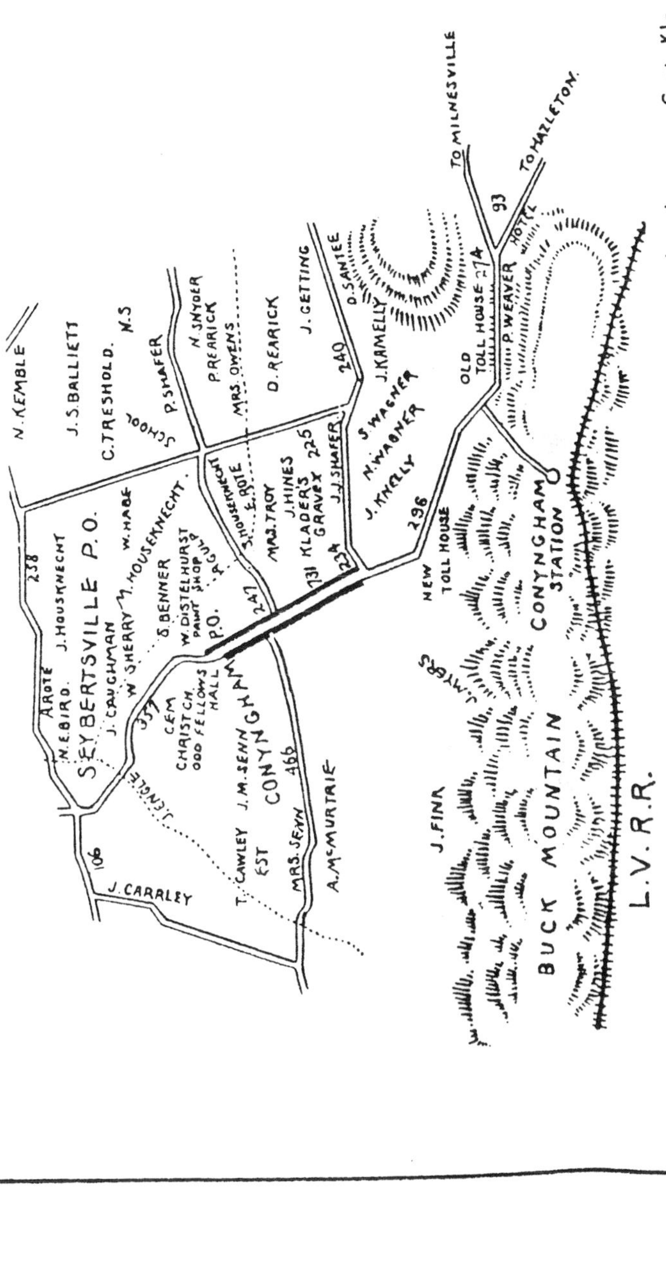

Old map of the Sugarloaf Massacre. It appears in the same Historical Record mentioned in the story. Capt. Klader's grave is marked with an X just above the name J.J. Shafer. It is near the site of the historical marker.

Chapter Four

THE SHADOW OF DEATH: SEPTEMBER 11, 1780

Captain Klader awoke his men before dawn. After a morning meal and a weapons' inspection the detachment broke camp and proceeded into the Hazle Swamp. The Moravian missionary Hackwelder Mack is thought to have been the first to call the area the "Haselschwamp," a name borrowed from the Indians themselves. The Moravians had utilized the Nescopeck Path since 1742 when Count Nicholas Ludwig Von Zinzendorf, the missionary founder of Bethlehem, first used the trail. The path widened in the shallow valley of the Hazle Swamp before continuing on to the Susquehanna River.

Klader was aware that he was moving into potentially hostile country, but he was unaware of any direct threat to his command. The detachment moved through the dense thickets in the area of the Upper Hazle Creek. They were probably the first white men to pass through what is today Hazleton, Pennsylvania. Klader's men moved roughly along the same route that Broad Street in Hazleton follows today. By mid-morning they were at the Black Creek. Before noon Klader's men were poised to surmount the Buck Mountain. Below them stretched the beautiful Sugarloaf Valley.

Klader did not know that Roland Montour's war party, notified by fleeing Tory sympathizers that a detachment of militia was coming, stealthily moved to engage him. Montour's thirty warriors moved east by Knob Mountain, passed Fort Wyoming undetected, and crossed the Susquehanna River at the mouth of the Nescopeck Creek. They followed the Nescopeck to its junction with the Little Nescopeck Creek, then followed it to near the Buck Mountain. Montour placed his men under cover in a pine grove, then awaited the arrival of his prey.[1]

Klader proceeded down the ravine following a brook until he came to a spring surrounded with thickets of bushes and trees densely over-grown with grapevines. A few of his more experienced men noticed that the Little Nescopeck appeared muddy, perhaps indicating some recent and unknown human presence. The men, bone-weary from the expedition and sweltering beneath the summer sun, sought refreshment and began to relax. It was around noon on September 11, 1780.

Captain Klader was somewhat disburdened by the fact that the valley's loyalist inhabitants had offered no resistance. Perhaps they had abandoned the valley altogether. Detecting no immediate threat to his men, Klader succumbed to a false sense of security.

Klader's men began to unsling their knapsacks. Some of the men stacked arms while others rested their weapons against rocks or trees. A number of weapons were carelessly abandoned on the ground. The men cleaned dirt and pebbles from their shoes, lay in the sun, smoked clay pipes, ate lunch. A few men climbed trees picking wild grapes from enveloping vines. Klader's detachment was now completely vulnerable, seemingly entranced in a strange euphoria.

Montour took the measure of his foe. He and Lieutenant Johnston counted but thirty-three militiamen (there were forty-one), and knowing he had thirty men, contemplated his next move. Some of the young-bloods were in favor of a headlong assault out of the pine grove and into the field where Klader's men relaxed beneath the midday sun. Other braves, more interested in plunder, were in favor of a strategic withdrawal. Montour decided upon a middle course. It was agreed that they would edge closer to the militiamen and unleash a volley of musket fire into the American position. If the militiamen were not quickly routed, Montour would withdraw his force to a designated rally point further up the Little Nescopeck Creek.[2]

Montour's men opened up on the unsuspecting Americans. Panic ensued. The hills resounded with furious Indian war whoops. In a flash the Senecas emerged from cover brandishing their tomahawks and engaged the militia in fierce hand-to-hand combat. Quickly seizing the discarded American muskets the Senecas rendered their foe virtually powerless. One soldier, still up a tree feasting on grapes, was shot down. He fell with a heavy thud to the ground. Men began to run in all directions.

The militiamen fought back with what arms they still had. Klader set a fine example demonstrating personal gallantry, but it was not enough. Eventually overpowered by several Indians, the young Captain was slowly tortured to death. Upon Klader's capture, Lieutenant John Myer assumed command of the shattered remnants of the detachment. Myer did what he could to rally the men. He seized his musket and swore that he would die before retreating. Ensign James Scoby and Private Peter Tubalt Coans rallied to his side, but most of the men were now either in full retreat, or had already fallen on the field. Montour was shot in the arm and badly wounded. At least one of the Senecas was killed. But the day belonged to the British. Montour's warriors took the three men prisoner.

While the battle raged, soldiers without their muskets attempted to escape. One tried to make it back up the ravine of Buck Mountain. His head was split open by a Seneca tomahawk. Private Henry Davis escaped over the Nescopeck Mountain and somehow got across the Susquehanna River to the ruins of Fort Jenkins. Yet another man escaped over the Buck Mountain leaving the Indian trail to his right and keeping out of sight of the Indians, who he could hear beating the brush behind him. By September 20, twenty-two of Klader's detachment of forty-one men had managed to reach safety.[3]

Fifteen Americans died on that bloodstained field beside the Little Nescopeck Creek. All of the dead were stripped naked, their bodies mutilated and scalped. Their corpses lay prostrate on that field for six days exposed to the elements and the wild animals. Along with Captain Daniel Klader, the American dead included Corporal Samuel Bond, and Privates Jacob Arndt, Peter Croom, Philip George, Abraham Klader, John Kouts, James McGraw, Paul Neely, George Peter Renhart, Jacob Row, George Shilhamer, Abraham Smith, Baltzer Snyder and John Weaver. Lieutenant John Myer, Ensign James Scoby and Private Peter Tubalt Coans were taken prisoner. The captives were to be conveyed to Fort Niagara. Montour's war party followed the Little Nescopeck to the Nescopeck Creek. From there they moved north towards the Susquehanna River. Klader's mission had ended in carnage.

Roland Montour was no stranger to combat. In 1778 he had commanded a force of three hundred warriors heading for Shamokin, Pennsylvania. They would later participate in the Wyoming Massacre which devastated the Yankee colony along the Susquehanna River. When Sullivan's expedition progressed into Iroquoia the following year, Montour offered brief but fierce resistance.[4]

On August 12, 1779 a band of hostile Delawares under the command of Montour held up a contingent of General Edward Hand's men under the command of Lieutenant Colonel Adam Hubley as they advanced upon Chemung. As Hubley's forward guard arrived at Chemung a dense mist obscured the river from their view. The village itself was deserted save for a sleeping dog. Campfires still burned. Hand ordered Hubley to advance through the village. Cowbells were heard. Hand was convinced that the enemy was nearby. Hubley's men rushed to where they thought the enemy was hiding, but ran instead into a deadly ambush planned by Montour himself. Montour and twenty Delaware Indians opened fire from concealed positions upon Hubley's hapless men. Six of Hubley's men were killed. Nine more were wounded. Had Hubley's men not been so widely dispersed Montour would have done even more damage. Hubley attempted to flank Montour's position. Seeing the danger, the wily Montour withdrew and vanished from sight.

By the time of the Sugarloaf Massacre a year later, Montour was battle-hardened, cunning and shrewd. He was a master of guerilla tactics. Well suited for the kind of terror campaign the British favored on the thinly populated frontier after their disaster at Saratoga, Montour was a most deadly foe.

In 1780, Montour was seemingly everywhere. Leaving Fort Niagara for the spring campaign as early as February, he was responsible for the capture of the Gilbert and Peart families near the Mahoning Creek in April. He participated in numerous raids in Pennsylvania throughout the spring and summer and was considered by the British to be one of their most reliable officers. He was given the rank of Captain and was often referred to as either "Chief Montour" or "Captain Montour." On September 6, he took part in the attack on Fort Rice and later burned Fort Jenkins.[5]

Montour was the son of the legendary Queen Esther, a Seneca leader who had figured prominently in the Wyoming Massacre. Queen Esther personally dispatched several captives with her tomahawk. She became known as the "fiend of Wyoming." Queen Esther's Town marked the south door of the Iroquois longhouse, and was situated near Teaga, Pennsylvania. Both towns were destroyed by Colonel Thomas Hartley and his troops on September 27, 1778. Queen Esther's Flats provided fine grazing land for livestock. The names of Montoursville, Pennsylvania, and Montour County itself, remind the discerning of this loyalist family.

Roland Montour was a great-grandson of Madame Montour, who held great power among the Iroquois during the first half of the eighteenth century. She was the daughter of a French nobleman named Montour who had settled in Canada around 1665. He took an Indian woman as his wife and fathered three children with her, two daughters and a son. In 1709, the son was killed by order of Governor Vaudreuil, for supposedly hampering trade beyond Montreal with the Indians. Madame Montour was captured by the Iroquois around 1694 when she was ten years of age. She later married a Seneca who became known as Roland Montour. At least four children were born to them: Andrew, Robert, Lewis and Margaret. After her first husband died Madame Montour married an Oneida chief named Carondowanen, or "Big Tree." He was also known as Robert Hunter. In 1729, Hunter was captured and killed by the Catawbas while on a war party.

Madame Montour came to hate the French for killing her brother. Her sister, who had married a Miami Indian, was used as a pawn by the French. They attempted to lure the Iroquois away from their alliance with the British. In 1727 Madame Montour was an interpreter at a peace council in Philadelphia where she received compliments for her culture, polish, refinement, and "other qualities."[6]

Count Von Zinzendorf visited her at Ostonwakin, near the mouth of the Loyalsock Creek in 1742. He also met her son Andrew Montour whom he described in his journal. Von Zinzendorf wrote that "Andrew's cast of countenance is decidedly European, and had not his face been encircled with a broad band of paint, applied with bear's fat, I would certainly have taken him for one. He wore a brown broadcloth coat, a scarlet damasken lapel-waistcoat, breeches, over which his shirt hung, a black Cordovan neckerchief, decked with silver bugles, shoes and stockings, and a hat. His ears were hung with pendants of brass and other wires plaited together like the handle of a basket. He was very cordial, but on addressing him in French, he, to my surprise, replied in English."[7]

Andrew Montour served as an interpreter and as a messenger for many years. In May 1745 he traveled with Conrad Weiser to Onondago. He seemed to be present as an interpreter at every council with the Indians. In 1752 he was given permission to select a residence for himself. He chose one hundred forty-three acres of Perry County farmland. In 1761 he was granted fifteen hundred acres on the Kishacoquillas Creek. Known as both Andrew and "Henry" Montour, he was with General Braddock's ill-fated expedition in 1755. Montour worked tirelessly as an interpreter and in his day, traveled nearly everywhere east of the Mississippi River. In 1769 he was granted another tract of land, three hundred acres which included Montour's Island, near Pittsburgh. Andrew Montour died much lamented on Montour's Island in 1789. As he gained fame as an interpreter, his niece Queen Esther became demonized. Roland Montour's public image would closely mirror that of his infamous mother.

Once caught in Montour's trap, Klader's men had little recourse. They had let down their guard for a few brief moments and then paid a horrendous price for it. After three days in the wilderness, most of it spent hiking through forbidding terrain, the detachment came to the open field by the Little Nescopeck. Captain Klader's men had marched well, but were clamoring to be briefly indulged before moving on again towards Berwick and Catawissa. Montour seized upon Klader's brief indulgence, exposed it as a terrible miscalculation, and wreaked havoc on the American position. A few moments of rest and relaxation cost fifteen men their lives.

The soldiers who noticed that the spring water was muddied, thereby indicating that it might have been recently stirred by an unknown human presence were overruled by other voices wanting a break. Perhaps, some reasoned, a bear or some other animal had been in the water, thus causing it to become muddy. Those voices urging caution were overruled. The men of Klader's detachment paid a terrible price for their nonchalance. For nearly a week, fifteen grotesque corpses remained on that field, decomposing beneath the fierce rays of the summer sun. Each evening the moon appeared, bathing the hideous spectacle in pale moonlight.

Chapter Five

BALLIET'S DETAIL

Montour's war party did not abandon the battlefield quickly. Elements of Klader's detachment ran as far as a thousand feet along the Little Nescopeck Creek before being killed. The Indians broke into several pursuing groups and furiously trailed after the fleeing remnants of the militia for several hours. They met with mixed success. As evening loomed the weary Senecas encamped some distance away from the killing ground. Exhausted from the battle and the hours of chase, carrying their dead, nursing their wounded, they secured the three prisoners - Myer, Scoby and Coans - then turned in for the night. Somewhere out in the bush, now beyond the Buck Mountain, or the Nescopeck Mountain, alone and in small numbers, the beleaguered remnants of Klader's command faced a night of anxiety and fear. Eventually reaching safety, they would relate their tales of death in the Pennsylvania wilderness.

No only was Roland Montour wounded, but Lieutenant Myer was also. The harrowing hand-to-hand fighting had left few unscathed. The next day the war party broke camp and followed the Nescopeck Path to the Susquehanna River.

The summer of 1780 was noted for its intense heat. August was referred to as having been "panting hot." September was little better. Severe thunderstorms were frequent as was the oppressive humidity. Fever gripped the settlements along the Susquehanna River. William H. Smith, a physician practicing along the Susquehanna, had many fever patients that summer. He treated them with calomel, tartar emetic, and "Jesuit's bark." Smith rarely lost a patient.[1]

On September 13, Montour's war party was in action again. Having returned to the Susquehanna River with their three prisoners and what spoils of war they had taken from the militiamen, they moved on to Harvey's Creek. They burned Benjamin Harvey's saw mill and several grain stacks in the vicinity. Lieutenant Myer managed to slip away

45

from his captors the previous night, but was unable to secure the release of Scoby and Coans. As Montour's men rampaged along the Susquehanna, Myer carefully made his way to Fort Wyoming. He arrived there on the 14th, emaciated and exhausted. Myer reported to the Commanding Officer, Colonel Zebulon Butler. As Myer spoke to Colonel Butler, Montour's war party crossed the Shawanese Mountain. They followed the Susquehanna north into New York and proceeded to Fort Niagara.

Lieutenant John Jenkins, Jr., recorded the arrival of Lieutenant John Myer at Fort Wyoming in his journal. He wrote that on Thursday, September 14, "Lieutenant Myers, from Fort Allen, came into the fort, and said he had made his escape from the Indians the night before, and that he had been taken in the Scotch Valley, and that he had thirty-three men with him, which he commanded. He was surrounded by the Indians, and thirteen of his men killed, and three taken. This day we heard that Fort Jenkins and Harvey's Mills were burnt."[2]

Jenkins had served as a guide to General Sullivan in the march from the Wyoming Valley to the Genesee River in 1779. A veteran of the Battle of Newtown, he became an influential politician in Northeastern Pennsylvania after the war. This account of the statement made by Myer to Colonel Butler raises questions. It is known that Captain Klader was in command of forty-one men, not thirty-three. The Jenkins' journal entry also suggests that Myer was in command at some point during the engagement, perhaps when Klader was among the thirteen Americans that lay dead or dying on the ground. Another two men were hunted down and dispatched by pursuing Indians as they fled from the killing ground. Fifteen of Klader's men were eventually listed as killed in action.

Colonel Zebulon Butler was aghast at Myer's report. Foodstuffs and other provisions were already in short supply at the fort. Now it was necessary to prepare for a possible attack from hostile Indians. On September 4, apparently unaware of the battle brewing at Fort Rice, Butler wrote to Colonel Ephraim Blaine, Commissary General of Purchases for the Continental Army in Philadelphia. "The intent of this is to apply to you to give order to Mr. (William) Stewart, Commissary of Issues at this post, or some purchasing commissary that will furnish him beef cattle or salt provision for the use of this garrison. He left this (place) by my order the 29th of last June to procure provisions for this garrison. We have been out of provisions near half the time since, and he has not returned. He has sent some flour, but not meat, and that I must send express to Colonel Blaine to furnish him with order or money, as he cannot procure it.

This express waits on you on purpose to have some relief for this garrison, which is a frontier, and ought to have at least three month's provisions on hand. With respect to flour, I think a supply may soon be had here, as there is a quantity of wheat to be sold here, and a mill will be ready to go in four or five weeks: but at present no person is authorised to purchase.

My making this application to you is by request of Mr. Stewart, Issuing Commissary at this post. If it should be out of the rule you'll please to excuse me; but so much is fact - we are out of provisions, and no prospect of getting meat. An answer by the bearer (Hugh Forseman) who awaits upon you will much oblige your humble servant."[3]

The burial detail left Fort Allen on the 15th and arrived at the battlefield two days later. Commanded by Lieutenant Colonel Stephen Balliet of the Northampton County Militia, with Colonel Kern of the Third Battalion and Colonel Giger of the Sixth, the detail took two days to arrive on the scene. They dug a mass grave for the victims of the massacre. The flesh of the cadavers was so putrid that tree branches and blankets were improvised to carry the dead to their final resting place. They were buried in the field where they fell. Captain Klader was buried beneath a nearby oak tree. One of the soldiers in the burial detail carved Klader's initials "D.K.," into the tree trunk.

The battlefield was still littered with debris despite the fact that the Senecas had carried off just about everything of material value. Bent and broken gun barrels, some with British markings, were taken by the men. The surrounding grass and weeds were still beaten down. After a religious ceremony ordered by Colonel Balliet, the burial detail trekked homewards. They arrived back at Fort Allen on the 19th.

While Balliet was leading his men back to Fort Allen, Colonel Blaine finally replied to Colonel Butler's request for provisions. Blaine wrote on September 18, that "I delayed your Express several days, expecting to obtain money or some other means to procure supplies of provisions. Under the present system the states are to furnish the supplies of our army. They have been so exceedingly dilatory that the army have been for several days, at different periods, without one morsel of meat of any kind, and are now in the most disagreeable situation for want of that article. I haven't it in my power, for the present, to give you any assistance but that of flour."[4]

As Blaine wrote his pathetic letter to Colonel Butler, the Seneca Chief Roland Montour died of wounds sustained at the Sugarloaf Massacre. Shot in the arm, Montour's wound had turned sceptic. Gangrene set in. Montour died on the 18th. Two days later Balliet wrote to General Joseph Reed, President of the Supreme Executive Council of Pennsylvania, informing him of recent events on the frontier. Montour's war party, with Ensign Scoby and Private Coans in tow, arrived at Fort Niagara a few days later.

Roland Montour was buried in the traditional manner of the Iroquois. Considered by the British and the Iroquois to have been one of their most reliable warriors, Montour received full honors.

On August 24, 1779 at Tioga, Lieutenant Beatty of Sullivan's command observed an Iroquois cemetery containing around one hundred graves. He wrote that "they bury their dead very curious, after this manner. They dig a hole the length of the person they are to bury and about two feet deep. They lay him on his back in the grave, with an old blanket or blanket coat round him, and lay bark over the grave, even with the surface of the earth, so as to prevent the earth from touching the body, then they heap up the dirt on the top of the grave in a round heap which is from four to six feet high."[5] Some Iroquois burials were done with the deceased in a sitting posture. The Seneca tribe sometimes relied upon ossuaries.

When the Seneca Chief Hiakatoo, the husband of Mary Jemison, died in November 1811 at the age of one hundred three, he was buried with all the insignia of a veteran warrior. A war club, tomahawk, scalping knife, powder flask, flint, a small cake, and a cup were placed in his coffin. Proudly arrayed in his best clothing, Hiakatoo went to the beyond with two or three candles to light his way. His coffin was then closed and carried to the grave.

Montour was buried in a similar fashion. As his body was lowered into the grave, Montour's spirit was addressed by a Seneca sachem. Montour was charged not to be troubled about himself in his new situation, nor on his journey and not to trouble his friends, wife or children, whom he had left behind. The sachem told him that if he met strangers on his way, to inform them what tribe he belongs to, who his relatives are, the situation in which he left them and that having done that he must keep on until he reached the good fields in the country of Hawaneu. The Senecas believed that when they reached Hawaneu they would see all of their ancestors and personal friends gone before them. They would join with the great leaders of their tribe to embrace Montour with deep affection and joy. Despite the promise of happiness in the afterlife the Iroquois generally felt great sadness when they lost one of their own.

In the first evening of the burial rite Montour's closest relatives built a fire at the head of his grave and sat near it until morning. They did this for nine consecutive nights. It was thought that the deceased ended his long journey to Hawaneu at the end of ten days.

Colonel Samuel Roy, having received notification from Colonel Balliet of recent events near the Little Nescopeck Creek, recorded that "Colonel Balliet informs me that he had given a counsel a relation of the killed and wounded he had found and buried near Nescopeck. As he was at the place of action, his account must be as near the truth as any that I could procure, though since Lieutenant Myers who was taken prisoner by the enemy in that unhappy action, has made his escape from the savages and reports that Ensign Scoby and one private were taken with him and that the party consisted of thirty Indians and one white savage; that they had thirteen scalps along with them; that several of them were wounded, and supposes some killed."[6]

Conditions on the frontier throughout 1780 were severe. Not only was the weather quite extreme for much of the year, but constant raids from the Indians and other British forces combined with a lack of provisions to make life miserable for the men garrisoning the frontier forts of New York and Pennsylvania. The autumn of 1780 was a time of great privation.

General Washington, in a letter written from his headquarters near Hackensack, New Jersey, to the Executive Council of Massachusetts on September 12, wrote that "I am pained to inform your Honorable body that our distresses for meat still continue pressing and alarming. The supplies we have received, including the cattle which have been exacted from the inhabitants of the state - and in many instances to their entire ruin - and which have made no inconsiderable part have been little more than sufficient to satisfy a third of our necessary demands. The troops on some occasions have been even four and five days without a mouthful of meat. Complaints and murmurings - a relaxation of discipline - marauding - robbery and desertion are the consequences; and, indeed, it is to be wondered at, that they have not prevailed to a much greater extent. I am satisfied things cannot continue long in their present condition."[7]

The timing of Klader's mission seems to have been inauspicious indeed. Pro-British forces were wreaking havoc throughout New York and Pennsylvania, while the American army's food supply was running critically low. Had Klader's men survived to reach Fort Wyoming they would have subsisted on meager rations with the rest of Colonel Butler's command.

Hugh Forseman wrote of this time in a petition presented to the Connecticut Assembly in October 1781. "The garrison at Wyoming was in August and September, 1780 much straitened and distressed for the want of provisions, by reason that Governor Reed prohibited its being bought from the Pennsylvania Purchasing Commissaries. While in this situation Colonel Zebulon Butler, who commanded the garrison, appointed and directed me to purchase provisions for the use of the troops - which appointment I received, September 20, 1780."[8]

On October 8, 1780 Colonel Butler wrote to William Stewart to inform him that "the boat with flour came. The meat was expended, and part of the flour. The two cattle likewise came, but we are entirely out of bread and meat. We live on eels and corn, and the eels seem to be the most done."[9] Five days later Colonel Hunter of Fort Augusta temporarily stopped the boats from ascending the Susquehanna River with provisions for Fort Wyoming. He was determined to send the grain to Stroudsburg for milling. This inexplicable action made life at Fort Wyoming even more miserable.

On October 19, 1780, Forseman wrote to Colonel Butler that he would remain in the city of Philadelphia until he received victualing orders from Colonel Blaine. Forseman finally arrived at Fort Wyoming on the 27th with one hundred head of cattle. Starvation had been narrowly avoided.

While frontier raids continued in Pennsylvania that October, Tryon County, New York, was devastated by Sir John Johnson. Leading his Royal Yorkers, a detachment of redcoats, along with Butler's Rangers, Johnson marched into the county from Fort Niagara and laid it waste. Johnson also commanded a contingent of two hundred sixty-five Iroquois which included Sayenqueraghta, Cornplanter and Joseph Brant. There were also some Cayugas under Chief Hung Face and some Tuscaroras under Sagwarithra. Entering the area by way of Oswego they moved south, then north, descending on the Schoharie settlement. The army smashed through the settlement, completely destroying it.

From there Johnson's army turned upon the settlement of Stone Arabia on the Mohawk River. Forts Ann and George were seized by the British invading from Canada. American settlements were burned in portions of Charlotte County and also Saratoga. The town of Ballston, a few miles northwest of Albany, was torched. As Johnson began to withdraw, hotly pursued by New York militiamen and pro-American Oneidas, the frontier region of New York was devastated.

Johnson's men returned to Fort Niagara triumphant, having inflicted a terrible blow to American interests in New York.

On November 19, a detachment of nineteen members of Butler's Rangers and five Indians left Fort Niagara on a final war party before winter set in. Commanded by Lieutenant John Turney, Sr., they began a marauding expedition along the Susquehanna River. The British arrived at the summit of the Shawanese Mountain, overlooking the Plymouth Township settlement in the afternoon of Wednesday, December 6, twenty-two days after leaving Fort Niagara.

Lieutenant John Jenkins recorded that on that morning "a party of tories and Indians took some prisoners from Shawwanee - (west of the river, two miles below Wilkes Barre). Did no other damage, except taking a small quantity of plunder. A party of our men sent after them, and pursued them three days, and gave out." The year 1780 ended as violently as it began.

Three months after the Sugarloaf Massacre the fear of further Indian attacks continued to alarm the settlers of Northeastern Pennsylvania and New York. Tales of frontier kidnappings, killings, mayhem and robbery, continued to be news. No major attack was made on Fort Wyoming, and the autumn harvest, despite being reduced by the severe heat of the past summer, was brought in.

The 1780 campaign had ravaged New York and Pennsylvania. Three hundred thirty Americans had been killed or taken prisoner, fourteen of whom were officers. Six forts and several mills had been destroyed. More than seven hundred homes and barns were burned, and nearly as many cattle driven off. Tons of grain had been destroyed. Terror gripped the Iroquois frontier. The economy of New York was strained to the breaking point. Pennsylvania's economic fortunes were little better. The Iroquois campaign of retribution which followed Sullivan's punitive campaign of 1779 had been a British success. The winter of 1780-1781 would be as severe as its predecessor had been. Once again the killing fields of the Iroquois frontier were frozen and snow covered for what seemed like an eternity.

The Sugarloaf Massacre Memorial, Sugarloaf, PA.

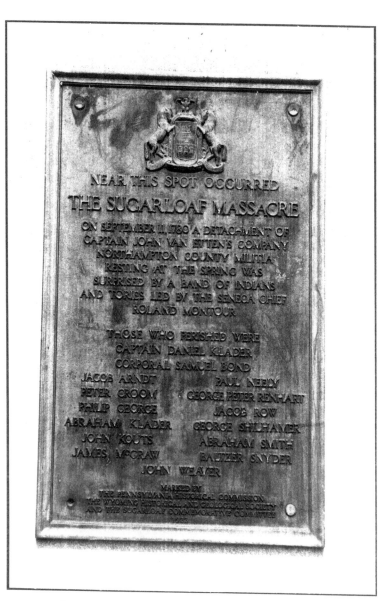

NEAR THIS SPOT OCCURRED

THE SUGARLOAF MASSACRE

ON SEPTEMBER 11, 1780 A DETACHMENT OF
CAPTAIN JOHN VAN ETTEN'S COMPANY
NORTHAMPTON COUNTY MILITIA
RESTING AT THE SPRING WAS
SURPRISED BY A BAND OF INDIANS
AND TORIES LED BY THE SENECA CHIEF
ROLAND MONTOUR

THOSE WHO PERISHED WERE
CAPTAIN DANIEL KLADER
CORPORAL SAMUEL BOND

JACOB ARNDT	PAUL NEELY
PETER CROOM	GEORGE PETER RENHART
PHILIP GEORGE	JACOB ROW
ABRAHAM KLADER	GEORGE SHILHAMER
JOHN KOUTS	ABRAHAM SMITH
JAMES McGRAW	BALTZER SNYDER

JOHN WEAVER

MARKED BY
THE PENNSYLVANIA HISTORICAL COMMISSION
THE WYOMING HISTORICAL AND GEOLOGICAL SOCIETY
AND THE SUGARLOAF COMMEMORATIVE COMMITTEE

Bronze Plaque, Sugarloaf Massacre Memorial.

Gravestone of Captain Daniel Klader, near massacre site.

The Pine Grove. In the foreground, the "bloodstained field."

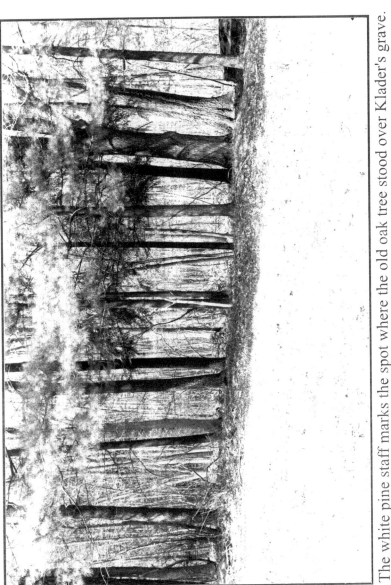

The white pine staff marks the spot where the old oak tree stood over Klader's grave.

Close-up of the spot where Klader is buried.
His men lie nearby in a common grave.

The Little Nescopeck Creek at Conyngham, PA.

The Little Nescopeck Creek flows towards
the "Big Nescopeck."

Chapter Six

FRONTIER ENDGAME: 1781-1783

Despite the severity of the weather, Indian attacks continued throughout the winter of 1780-1781. In 1781, sixty-four war parties left Fort Niagara bound for frontier settlements in New York, Pennsylvania and Ohio. These raids concentrated primarily on targets that had been hit in the previous year. Settlers had their newly rebuilt buildings destroyed again by the Iroquois. Other raids focused on fresh targets of opportunity.[1]

Joseph Brant attacked the German Flats settlement in January 1781. That month Chief Philip Hough led a group of fourteen Delawares to the Hudson River. On January 15, the Mohawk David Karaghqunty followed up on Hough's attack and devastated the area. Two days later Captain Shinop led nine Nanticokes on a raiding expedition into the Susquehanna Valley.

Scalps continued to be prized by both sides. On February 19, Colonel Archibald Lochry, the Lieutenant of Westmoreland County, Pennsylvania, was ordered to pay the sum of twelve pounds, ten shillings, state money, to Captain Samuel Brady "as a reward for an Indian's scalp."[2]

During the 1781 campaign sixty-four Indian war parties consisting of nearly three thousand warriors took to the field. Most of the war parties were small, but they traveled swiftly, struck ferociously, and made frontier life a precarious misery for many Americans throughout the year.

The Mohawk Captain David Hill led a war party of eighty-three men into the field that spring. He was accompanied by Lieutenant Brown of the Indian Department. They attacked settlers around Fort Pitt. Chew Tobacco took twenty-two braves and moved toward Fort Pitt, inflicting what damage he could. Captain John Deserontyon, in command of forty-four warriors, most of whom were Tuscaroras,

61

ravaged the Canajoharie district and the Mohawk. Throughout the spring of 1781 raids continued. Minisink, Currietown, Cherry Valley, and Shamokin were all hit. The Indians inflicted severe damage on the Delaware, Mohawk, Ohio and Susquehanna River valleys as well.[3]

Joseph Brant, with seventeen warriors, left Fort Niagara in April for the Shawnee country along the Ohio River. He remained there until late summer. Brant burned one hundred two houses, four forts, sixty granaries and ten mills. He seized three hundred twenty-seven cattle and horses. Fifty-four Americans were killed and one hundred forty-three were taken prisoner. The Ohio Valley was in flames.

Captain Moses Van Campen seemed to be everywhere on the Pennsylvania frontier during those turbulent years. In the spring of 1781 he helped erect Fort McClure at Bloomsburg. Situated on the north bank of the Susquehanna River, it was designed to protect settlers after the destruction of Fort Jenkins in 1780. That summer a report came in to Colonel Hunter at Fort Augusta that as many as three hundred Iroquois were massing north of the Sinnemahoning Creek in North-Central Pennsylvania.

Hunter quickly assembled a reconnaissance force. It consisted of Van Campen, Captain Campbell, Lieutenant Cramer and two brothers, Peter and Michael Grove. The team became known as the "Grove Party." The men chosen for this dangerous mission into hostile country were considered to be the best frontiersmen available. They would have to be.

The Grove Party came upon an Iroquois war party of about thirty braves lying by a campfire. Waiting until the Indians were asleep, Van Campen and his men edged closer to the camp under the cover of night. They rushed in, killing several sleeping warriors with their own rifles and tomahawks. A number of Indians fled into the forest. Van Campen's men found a number of scalps and a sizeable quantity of cloth. They gave the latter to needy families around Fort Augusta.

In the spring of 1782, Van Campen was engaged with others in rebuilding Fort Muncy, which had been destroyed by the Iroquois in

1779. Fort Muncy was located about five miles from the town of Muncy in Lycoming County, Pennsylvania. On April 10, Van Campen led a group of twenty men into the wilderness to ascertain the validity of rumors coming in of renewed Indian atrocities in the area. By the 15th, Van Campen's party had moved past the "Great Island" in the Susquehanna (near Lock Haven), to Bald Eagle Creek. They were attacked there by a war party of eighty-five Indians. Only three Americans escaped the fury of the Iroquois. Nine of Van Campen's party were killed, the rest taken captive. Moses Van Campen was now a prisoner.

The Iroquois carried their captives to the Seneca village of Caneadea on the Genesee River. Van Campen and his men were forced to run the gauntlet. The feisty frontiersman survived this ordeal, as did about half of the captives with him. The battered survivors were adopted into Seneca families. Van Campen was not. He was taken to Fort Niagara and handed over to the British. They interrogated him and at one point attempted to cajole him into joining their cause. He would not budge. "No sir, no," said Van Campen, "my life belongs to my country. Give me the stake, tomahawk, or the scalping knife, but I will never dishonor the character of an American officer."[4] The British imprisoned him until March 1783 when he was released as part of a prisoner exchange. Moses Van Campen, the frontiersman and Indian fighter, died at home in 1849. He was ninety-two.

In New York, Fort Stanwix was abandoned by the Americans and the garrison relocated to Fort Herkimer. Forty Indians were killed in July when Colonel Marinus Willett defeated Chief Quackack, but in August the Iroquois struck back and burned Wawarsing in Ulster County.

On August 26 Joseph Brant, commanding one hundred warriors, defeated a detachment of General Clark's army under the command of Colonel Lochry. Lochry was on his way from Fort Pitt to Sandusky. Lochry, six officers and thirty privates were killed. The rest of his force was taken prisoner.

Major John Ross, in command of a British force of over six hundred men, departed Oswego on October 11. They reached Ganaghsaraga Creek four days later. Ross was joined there by a contingent of Iroquois. On October 17, he began taking prisoners. Ross arrived at the settlement of Warren's Bush in the early morning of October 25, having marched through a driving rainstorm. The town was burned. About one hundred farms were destroyed, along with three mills and a granary. Over twenty houses and ten barns were torched. Thousands of bushels of grain were ruined, and over two hundred cattle were slaughtered.

After this action, Ross decided upon a prudent course and began to move his troops towards Fort Niagara. He ordered his men to cross the Mohawk River. Colonel Willett arrived at the scene near Johnstown, New York. A battle broke out. Willett was reinforced by some sixty Oneidas. During the combat an Oneida brave slew Colonel Walter Butler. Accounts of the action vary. One account states that Butler's skull was split open with an Oneida tomahawk as he begged for quarter. His scalp was then taken. Another account states that he was simply shot through the head. Both stories agree that Butler was killed on the battlefield. As the British retreated the militia and the Oneidas pursued them, driving them back to Fort Niagara. The British expedition which had begun so successfully ended in a virtual rout.

Cornwallis surrendered to Washington at Yorktown on October 19, 1781. The Revolutionary War may have been over, but the frontier war with the Iroquois continued its savage pattern for several more months.

Lieutenant Adam Crysler, with twenty-eight Onoquaga Indians, attacked Schoharie on November 18, killing one man, burning two houses and driving off some fifty head of cattle. After this action they skirmished with some New York militiamen, killing five and wounding several others.

That fall, the Moravian settlement at Gnadenhuetten, not far from Fort Allen and the Lehigh River in Pennsylvania, was the scene of a savage massacre. The instigators of this action were not the Indians, but Americans themselves. Long known for their fair dealings with the Indians, these pacifists were accused by some of aiding and abetting the enemy. Ninety-six Moravian faithful were killed in cold blood by Colonel David Williamson's militiamen. This action even shocked the Iroquois.

Two months later the Indians exacted their revenge. Colonel William Crawford and the infamous Williamson were captured in the Ohio country. Crawford suffered a horrible death. He was scalped alive. Hot ashes were poured over his head. Crawford was then slowly roasted to death.[5]

Stunned by the barbarity of this action, Sir Guy Carleton effectively ended Great Britain's alliance with the Indians. In response to this, Pennsylvania eventually stopped paying money for scalps. Peace was beginning to dawn between the British and Americans, but the Iroquois themselves had little taste for it. Still smarting from Sullivan's Campaign in 1779 and impelled by their subsequent victories, many warriors desired to fight on.

The frontier war continued. In the spring of 1782, Captains Isaac Hill and John Deserontyon destroyed a mill at Little Falls, New York, near the Mohawk River. Sayenqueraghta, with three hundred warriors, advanced toward Wheeling. On June 18, Joseph Brant led three hundred Indians to Oswego. On July 5, his force now numbering four hundred sixty, Brant headed for the frontier. He was accompanied by the light infantry company formally under the command of Major John Ross. The would-be combatants were recalled in the field by a letter from General Haldimand. The war was winding down.

The last Indian attack in Luzerne County, Pennsylvania, is thought to have occurred on July 8, 1782. John Jameson, his brother Benjamin, and a neighbor named Asa Chapman left their homes in Hanover Township and rode towards Wilkes-Barre. They approached the church at "Hanover Green," which stood in a clearing. John Jameson noticed an Indian ambush ahead. After shouting out a warning he reared up in his horse and was struck three times by musket fire.

Jameson fell to the ground and his horse galloped away wildly. Jameson was later dispatched with a tomahawk and then scalped.

Asa Chapman and his horse were both wounded. Chapman's horse wheeled around and galloped for home, still carrying his slumped owner. Benjamin Jameson's horse also wheeled at first fire, and he was able to get home unscathed. The Indians, part of an Iroquois war party, vanished into the wilderness and into history.

Frontier skirmishes continued to occur in New York until February 1783. That month Colonel Willett attempted to seize the Oswego area from the British. Willett sent in an attack force from Canajoharie using sleighs. They crossed Oneida Lake on ice, but the Indian guides lost their way. The attack failed. Washington consoled Willett in a letter. The General wrote that there are at times "unaccountable Events, which are not within the controul of human means and which, tho' they often occur in military life, yet require not only the fortitude of the Soldier, but the calm reflection of the Philosopher, to bear."[6]

The Revolutionary War finally ended on September 3, 1783. Washington delivered his Farewell Address on November 2, and the following day Congress officially disbanded the Continental Army. The war which ravaged the frontier and pitted minuteman against redcoat, patriot against loyalist, also divided the Six Nations of the Iroquois Confederacy. While the British and Americans were able to effectively transcend the divisiveness of the war, the Iroquois were not so fortunate. The American Revolution created a destructive environment that proved toxic to the Iroquois. While the Canandaigua Treaty of 1794 brought peace between the United States and the Six Nations, it also sounded the death-knell of this proud native people.

The Sugarloaf Massacre of September 11, 1780 was one of a score of barbarous and ultimately futile actions carried out on the frontier during the war. After the fury of muskets and tomahawks finally abated, settlers entered the Sugarloaf Valley. The scenic valley dominated by the Sugarloaf Mountain became the cherished home of many.

Figure 5 (Map)   Sugarloaf Township, Pennsylvania

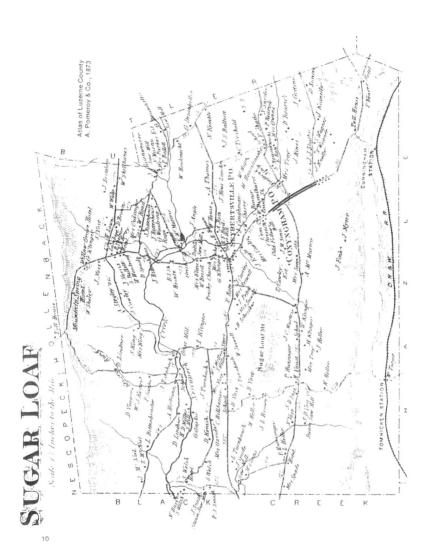

Chapter Seven

TURNIPS AND VENISON

The Sugarloaf Valley was permanently settled after the close of the Revolutionary War. Soldiers returning to Fort Allen after the burial detail of 1780, told of its beauty and charm. It was splendid country, amply suited for the yeoman's plough and the woodsman's axe.

Colonel Stephen Balliet's brother John, was the first white man to settle in the valley after the war.[1] The Balliet family arrived on horseback from Northampton County in 1784. They crossed over the Buck Mountain and followed the Indian path into the valley. The same trail was used four years earlier by Captain Klader's doomed expedition. The family settled near the present boundary between Butler and Sugarloaf Townships. The Balliet family soon had neighbors. Within a few years numerous families, most of them Pennsylvania Germans, entered the valley. George Drum, Henry Davis, Andrew Mowery and Philip Woodring were a few of these early pioneers.

The Osterdock, or "Easterday" family arrived after purchasing two hundred eighty-five acres of land from the Penn family in 1793. George Easterday named his new home in Sugarloaf "Georgia." He built a log cabin about one-half mile south of Conyngham near the foot of Buck Mountain. In 1804, the Lehigh and Susquehanna Turnpike was completed and a toll house erected near the Easterday property.

John Deiter Heller moved north from Northampton County and settled near Shamokin in 1789. Members of his family would figure prominently in the future development of the Sugarloaf Valley.

The first concern of these pioneers was survival. They worked hard, utilizing the axe and the plough, clearing the land and planting crops. Most of them built log cabins. Some also had a meat house. Christian Miller even had a stable. The cabins tended to have two floors and featured whitewashed walls, both inside and out. Oak planks replaced crude dirt floors. Chimneys were made of mountain stone, or creek stone, and were placed outside the cabin. The children usually slept upstairs while the adults slumbered below. A fireplace heated the cabin and cooked the food. Muskets and powder horns hung visibly over the fireplace. Iron pots, a kettle, deerskin pouches, and a Bible were to be found in nearly every home. Most families possessed at least two rifles.

The typical evening meal consisted of broiled venison or spare ribs, corn bread and honey, sweet potatoes, milk or water. A census taker working in the Sugarloaf Valley in 1820 remarked that the local inhabitants are mainly poor Germans living chiefly on turnips and venison.[2]

There were times when these early settlers went to bed hungry. Famine felled a number of these pioneers. The winters could be especially harsh. Stored provisions often ran low then and opportunities to hunt game were minimal. Settlers had little money to purchase goods and had to travel to Nescopeck if they wished to barter for them. One Sugarloaf resident killed a panther, then dragged its carcass into Columbia County to collect the $10.00 bounty.

Christian Miller arrived from Northumberland County in 1799. He built a log cabin, an outhouse, and stable, on three hundred acres of land located just east of the Sugarloaf Mountain. Much of Miller's land was dense forest and provided him with plenty of wild game. Miller died in 1821 at the age of ninety. George Drum, Bernard Hunsinger, William and David Rittenhouse, were also early Sugarloaf Valley pioneers and former residents of Northumberland County, Pennsylvania.

Anthony Weaver, a veteran of the Revolutionary War, became the first owner of the Sugarloaf Mountain. Weaver, a man known more for his ability to hold strong liquor than for his religious fervor, founded a family line that continues to proliferate in the valley today.

The pioneers were primarily common people of humble origin. They were considered to be honest, rough in their mannerisms, and unsophisticated. Alcohol was a common vice. In their love of strong drink the early residents of the Sugarloaf Valley mirrored eighteenth century American society itself. Samuel Adams was not the only "brewer patriot" in the country. Whisky, apple brandy, toddy, rum, cider, and strong ale were among the favorite libations of the period. Men prided themselves on their ability to handle strong drink. Some pioneer women were not above the occasional "nip" for "medicinal purposes."

Richard Allen built the first saw mill in the valley in 1798. By 1810, George Drum was operating a carding mill along the Little Nescopeck. The mill took locally raised wool and prepared the woolen fibers for spinning by hand. Drum's mill was located in the village of Asheville, now known as Fritzingertown. Three years later Samuel Woodring built a grist mill on the Nescopeck Creek, and in 1814 Redmond Conyngham added a grist mill to his saw mill on the Little Nescopeck. The development of these enterprises in the Sugarloaf Valley permitted the settlers to expand their horizons beyond the parameters necessitated by a subsistence economy.[3]

Grain was rafted down the Nescopeck Creek to the Susquehanna River and from there was sold to merchants who were free to send it to Philadelphia and beyond, using Durham boats. The settlers also conducted trade with their former neighbors in Northampton and Northumberland counties. Much of this business would have been conducted in German, but English was required for trade with the Wyoming Valley.

Circuit riding ministers of the German Reformed Church made the journey from Northampton County into the Sugarloaf Valley as early as 1790. In 1800, an energetic minister of this denomination, the Reverend John Mann, preached in the valley. Around this time the Reverend T. Klenner, a Lutheran minister, also shared the good news of the gospel in the valley. In 1809, the two German-speaking congregations united to build a church and school building which they shared for many years.

By 1830, a few hardy settlers who had once subsisted on "turnips and venison" laid the foundations of future prosperity. The sacrifice of Captain Daniel Klader's detachment would be greatly ennobled by the success of this thriving community.

The old battlefield has languished in relative obscurity for more than two centuries. During the 1850s some irreverent hand cut down the oak tree over Captain Klader's grave. In time even its roots rotted away. Joseph Fisher, an aged valley resident, toured the field some thirty years later with the editor of the "Hazleton Sentinel" newspaper. The two men could find no trace of Klader's grave, or the common grave where many of his men are buried. "As the old man leaned upon his staff ... he gave expression of deep regret that the tree was not permitted to stand as a memorial of the heroic deeds of those bygone days," the editor wrote.[1]

In 1914, Charles Rhoads Roberts wrote that well might they have exclaimed, who revered the name of the hero of Sugarloaf Valley,

> "Woodsman spare that tree!
> Touch not a single bough!"[2]

Abigail Dodson, who was captured by the Indians near the Mahoning Creek in the spring of 1780, was told the story of the Sugarloaf Massacre while in captivity. Her account of the massacre largely paralleled those of the survivors of Klader's detachment. Some of the veterans reported spotting a Tory with red hair, perhaps Lieutenant William Johnston of Butler's Rangers. The Sugarloaf Massacre Memorial and the Pennsylvania State Historical Marker serve to identify an important event in state history, first experienced, and later discussed, by the survivors themselves.

The debris scattered over the battlefield also had a tale to tell. Along with the mutilated, naked corpses of Klader's detachment, the burial detail found a new fuse on the ground and several bent and broken gun barrels. Some of them had British markings. One smoothbore gun, three other guns, and eleven rifles, with the appurtenance of thirteen soldiers were initially recorded as lost after the battle. Facts later revealed that "the appurtenances" had belonged to fifteen patriots rather than thirteen.

The fate of the two men who were taken to Fort Niagara after failing to escape with Lieutenant Myer is unknown. Ensign James Scoby and Private Peter Tubalt Coans did survive the perilous journey, and arrived at Niagara, but there is no apparent record of them after that. Scoby and Coans would almost certainly have been made to run a Seneca gauntlet. This gauntlet would have been rendered even more ferocious given that fact that Roland Montour had recently died of wounds suffered at Sugarloaf. The fate of these two men remains one of the mysteries of the Sugarloaf Massacre.

The dedication of the Sugarloaf Massacre Memorial proceeded on schedule, Saturday afternoon, September 9, 1933. A granite shaft was erected on land leased to the Pennsylvania Historical Commission by Charles H. Rice. A tablet containing a brief synopsis of the massacre and the names of the soldiers who perished was designed by Paul Cret, and cast in bronze by Bureau Brothers. A program was handed out to participants which included the text of the principal addresses.

The ceremony began at 2:00 p.m., with an introduction of the Chairman of the Day, the Honorable E. Foster Heller, Judge of the Orphan's Court for Luzerne County. Miss Frances Dorrance, Chairman of the Sugarloaf Commemorative Committee and Director of the Wyoming Historical and Geological Society, delivered the introduction.

An invocation was offered by the Reverend Allen H. Roth, Pastor of Christ Lutheran Church, Conyngham. Mrs. Raymond L. Wadhams, Regent of the Wyoming Chapter, Daughters of the American Revolution, dedicated the marker over the grave of Captain Daniel Klader. The audience then sang "America."

George S. Henritzy presented and raised the American flag. Joseph Hornick and George Novotnie, members of Hazleton Post Number 76, American Legion Drum and Bugle Corps, provided the bugle call to the colors. The national anthem was played by the Hazleton Liberty Band. As J. E. Altmiller conducted the band, nearly all of the participants, some of them quite visibly moved, sang along.

Milo Daniel Clader, a descendant of Captain Daniel Klader's brother Jacob, arose and delivered an address on the Klader family. He was followed by William Tilden Stauffer, President of the Thomas Nelson, Jr., Chapter, Sons of the American Revolution. Stauffer's address focused on the Sugarloaf Massacre itself. A patriotic selection was then performed by the Hazleton Liberty Band.

John H. Bonin, the Prothonotary of Luzerne County, introduced the Honorable Edward C. Shannon, the Lieutenant Governor of Pennsylvania. He was followed by Charles H. Rice, the donor of the memorial site. Rice presented the lease to Dr. James N. Rule, Chairman of the Pennsylvania Historical Commission. Rule accepted the lease on behalf of the historical commission and the people of Pennsylvania.

The memorial tablet was then unveiled by Marion Vaughn Markle, a descendant of the family that produced Private Henry Davis of Klader's detachment. After the unveiling, the audience stood as the Hazleton Liberty Band played "Roslin Castle." This lament was popular with regimental bands during the American Revolution. It was a mournful expression of respect for fallen comrades.

The ceremony ended with "Taps," played by Hornick and Novotnie. People tarried for awhile to examine the memorial and socialized before departing. One hundred fifty-three years after the Sugarloaf Massacre, a memorial honoring the sacrifice of Klader's detachments had finally been erected. A State Historical Marker was added a short distance away in 1947.

In 1976, a play about the massacre was performed. Part of the celebration pageant for the nation's Bicentennial, the production directed by Christopher Staudenmeier, featured Sugarloaf area adults and children in period costume. Among the characters portrayed were Madame Montour, Queen Esther, Sir William Johnson, General Sullivan, and Abigail Dodson. Blanche Ernst Hilliard served as the music chairman, and also accompanied a chorus which included sopranos, altos, tenors, and basses. It was a delightful performance. The Sugarloaf Massacre had once again been commemorated.

Two hundred twenty years have passed since that bloody encounter along the Little Nescopeck. The bloodstained field has again slipped back into obscurity. Few of today's Sugarloaf Valley residents are apparently aware that beneath the shadow of Buck Mountain fifteen veterans of the American Revolution sleep for eternity. The old battlefield at Sugarloaf is hallowed ground.

The words of Ralph Waldo Emerson's "Concord Hymn" invoke a profound image of that faraway day in 1780. They were read by William Tilden Stauffer at the dedication ceremony of the Sugarloaf Massacre Memorial in 1933.

"On this green sward, near this soft stream
We set today a votive stone;
That memory may their deeds redeem,
When like our sires, our sons are gone.
Spirit, that made those heroes dare
To die, and leave their children free,
Bid Time and Nature gently spare
The shaft we raise to them and thee."[3]

APPENDIX A

Letter from Lieutenant Colonel Stephen Balliet, of the First Battalion, Northampton County Militia, to Joseph Reed, President of the Supreme Executive Council.

Northampton County,
Septr. 20th, 1780.

Sir,

I take the earliest opportunity to acquaint your Excelency of the Distressed and Dangerous Situation of our frontier inhabitants, and the Misfortune Happened to our Volunteers stationed at the Gnaden Hutts.

They having Received Intelligence that a Number of Disaffected Persons lived near the Susquehanna at a place called the Scotch Valley, who have been suspected to hold up a correspondence with the Indians, and the Tories in the country. They sat out on the 8th Inst for that Place to see whether they might be able to find out anything of that nature, but they were attacked on the 10th at noon about 8 miles from that Settlement by a large Body of Indians and Torys (as one had Red hair). Supposed by some forty & by others twice that number they totally Dispersed our People, twenty-two out of forty-one have since come in several of whom are wounded.

It is also reported that Lieut. Jno. Meyer had been made prisoner and made his escape from them again and Returned at Wyoming.

On the first notice of this unfortuned event the officers of the militia have Exerted themselfs to get volunteers out of their Respective Divissions to go up and Buiry the Dead, their Labour Proved not in vain we collected about 150 men, officers Included from the Colonels Kern, Giger and my own Batallions, who would undergo the fatigue and danger to go there and pay that respect to their slautered

Bretheren, Due to men who fell in support of the freedom of their Country.

On the 15th we took up our line of march (want of ammunation Prevented us from going Sooner). On the 17th we arrived at the place of action, where we found Ten of our Soldiers Dead, Scalped, Striped Naked, and in a most cruel and barborous manner Tomehawked, their throates cut, etc., etc., whom we Buireed and Returned without even seeing any of these black alies, and bloody executors of British Tirany.

I can't Conclude without observing that the Colonels Kern of the 3d Battalion and Giger of the 6th who is upwards of sixty years of age, Together with all the other officers and men have encountered these High and many Hills and mountains with the greatest satisfaction and Discipline Imaginably, and their Countenances appeared to be Eager to engage with these tiranical enemy's who are employed by the British Court and aquipt at their Expence, as appeared by a new fusse, and several Gun Barrels etc., Bent and broke in pieces with the British Stamp, thereon, found by our men.

We also have great Reason to believe that several of the Indians have been killed by our men, in Particular by Col. Kern and another by Capt. Moyer, both of whom went Volunteers with this partie. We Viewed where they said they fired at them and found the grass and weeds Rimarkably beat down, though they had carried them off.

So I conclude with Remaining Your Excellency's most Humble servant,

Stephen Balliet
Lt. Colo. B.N.C.M.

Directed to Excellency Joseph Reed, Esqr. etc., Philadelphia.

APPENDIX B

Captain Van Etten's Company.

A muster roll of a company of volunteers, Northampton County, Pennsylvania, in the service of the United States, commanded by Johannes Van Etten, January 15, 1781.

Captain
Johannes (John) Van Etten, June 15, 1780.

First Lieutenant
John Fish, June 15, 1780.

Second Lieutenant
John Myer, June 15, 1780.

Ensigns
Henry Bush, June 15, 1780.
James Scoby, September 1, 1780;
taken prisoner 11th September.

Sergeants
Thomas Johnston, June 15, 1780.
Samuel Hellet, June 15, 1780.
James Scoby, June 15, 1780;
advanced to Ensign the 1st September.
Frederick Everhart, June 15, 1780.
Joseph Gable, August 30, 1780;
entered Sergeant.
George Price, July 15, 1780.

Corporals
Lewis Holmes, June 15, 1780.
Thomas Gay, June 15, 1780.
Samuel Bond, June 15, 1780;
killed 11th September.
Adam Hicker, July 17, 1780.

<u>Privates</u>

Samuel Vandermark, June 15, 1780.
Daniel McDole, June 15, 1780.
John Morhart, June 15, 1780.
John Kouts, June 15, 1780;
killed 11th September.
Rudolph Smith, June 17, 1780.
Abraham Klader, June 15, 1780;
killed 11th September.
Daniel Smith, June 17, 1780.
George Gongaware, June 17, 1780.
John Myer, June 15, 1780.
Peter Apler, June 15, 1780.
John Weaver, June 17, 1780;
killed 11th September.
Daniel France, July 8, 1780.
Lawrence Miller, July 8, 1780.
George Pigg, June 15, 1780.
John Robenholt, June 15, 1780.
Leonard Pack, June 15, 1780.
John Sack, June 15, 1780.
Job Stout, June 15, 1780.
George Ripsher, June 15, 1780.
Peter Snyder, June 15, 1780.
Peter Lasher, June 15, 1780.
Jacob Cryder, June 15, 1780.
Coanrode Kowler, June 15, 1780.
John Napsnyder, June 15, 1780.
Adam Teel, June 15, 1780.
Voluntine Nicholas, June 15, 1780.
George Hikman, June 15, 1780.
John Smith, June 15, 1780.
John Wetherstone, June 15, 1780.
Christian Haller, July 14, 1780.
Jacob Houser, July 30, 1780.
Peter Siner, July 30, 1780.
Peter Tubalt Coans, June 15, 1780;
taken prisoner 11th September.

Philip George Shilhamer, August 7, 1780.
Baltzer Snyder, July 5, 1780;
killed 11th September.
Philip Bitten, August 3, 1780;
deserted 10th November.
George Peter Renhart, June 28, 1780;
killed 11th September.
Andrew Myer, June 15, 1780.
Joseph Gable, July 3, 1780;
advanced to Sergeant 30th August.
Peter Croom, June 15, 1780;
killed 11th September.
Johannes Snyder, June 20, 1780.
Andrew Mourer, June 15, 1780.
Adam Lung, June 15, 1780.
George Shilhamer, August 17, 1780;
killed 11th September.
Paul Neely, July 18, 1780;
killed 11th September.
Abraham Smith, July 24, 1780;
killed 11th September.
John Lyn, June 15, 1780;
sick, absent.
Jacob Arndt, June 15, 1780;
killed 11th September.
Samuel Summeny, July 25, 1780.
Jacob Collens, June 15, 1780.
Henry Davis, June 15, 1780.
Philip George, June 15, 1780;
killed 11th September.
Peter McCoy, July 24, 1780.
John Haun, July 25, 1780.
Abraham Wisner, June 15, 1780.
Uriah Tippy, June 15, 1780.
Paul Reeser, June 15, 1780.
Ballser Wever, June 15, 1780.
George Heter, June 15, 1780.
John Smith, Jr., June 15, 1780.

Christian Wood, June 15, 1780.
John Morgan, June 15, 1780.
Henry France, June 15, 1780.
Bond Hewe, June 15, 1780.
John Hain, June 15, 1780.
Michael Yerty, June 15, 1780.
Adam Brunthaver, June 15, 1780.
Antony Bishop, June 15, 1780.
John Snider, June 15, 1780.
Peter Daniel, June 15, 1780.
Peter Simonton, June 15, 1780.
John Dayly, June 15, 1780.
Henry Van Garden, June 15, 1780.
Abraham Westfall, June 15, 1780.
Cornelius Devoor, June 15, 1780.
Casper Clutter, June 15, 1780.
Peter Quick, June 15, 1780.
Thomas Van Sikkle, June 15, 1780.
Samuel Van Garden, June 15, 1780.
Solomon Huff, June 15, 1780.
Thomas Hewe, June 30, 1780.
James McGraw, July 24, 1780;
killed 11th September.
Jacob Row, June 15, 1780;
killed 11th September.

The totle pay of the within company is neer abought £1906. I do sware that the within muster role is a true state of the company without froud to the United States or any Individual, to the best of my knoledg.

Johannes Van Etten, Captain.

Mustered at Fort Penn, January the fifteenth, 1781, in the absence of the muster master.

Jacob Stroud, Lieutenant Colonel.

The Canandaigua Treaty of 1794

PREAMBLE

A Treaty Between the United States of America and the Tribes Called the Six Nations:

The President of the United States having determined to hold a conference with the Six Nations of Indians for the purpose of removing from their minds all causes of complaint, and establishing a firm and permanent friendship with them; and Timothy Pickering being appointed sole agent for the purpose; and the agent having met and conferred with the sachems and warriors of the Six Nations in general council: Now, in order to accomplish the good design of this conference, the parties have agreed on the following articles, which, when ratified by the President, with the advice and consent of the Senate of the United States, shall be binding on them and the Six Nations....

ARTICLE 1. Peace and friendship are hereby firmly established, and shall be perpetual, between the United States and the Six Nations.

ARTICLE 2. The United States acknowledge the lands reserved to the Oneida, Onondaga, and Cayuga Nations in their respective treaties with the State of New York, and called their reservations, to be their property; and the United States will never claim the same, nor disturb them, or either of the Six Nations, nor their Indian friends, residing thereon, and united with them in the free use and enjoyment thereof; but the said reservations shall remain theirs, until they choose to sell the same to the people of the United States, who have the right to purchase.

ARTICLE 3. The land of the Seneca Nation is bounded as follows: beginning on Lake Ontario, at the northwest corner of the land they sold to Oliver Phelps; the line runs westerly along the lake, as far as

Oyongwongyeh Creek, at Johnson's Landing Place, about four miles eastward, from the fort of Niagara; then southerly, up that creek to its main fork, continuing the same straight course, to that river; (this line, boundary of a strip of land, extending from the same line to Niagara River, which the Seneca Nation ceded to the King of Great Britain, at the treaty held about thirty years ago, with Sir William Johnson); then the line runs along the Niagara River to Lake Erie, to the northwest corner of a triangular piece of land, which the United States conveyed to the State of Pennsylvania, as by the President's patent, dated the third day of March, 1792; then due south to the northern boundary of that State; then due east to the southwest corner of the land sold by the Seneca Nation to Oliver Phelps; and then north and northerly, along Phelps' line, to the place of beginning, on the Lake Ontario. Now, the United States acknowledge all the land within the aforementioned boundaries, to be the property of the Seneca Nation; and the United States will never claim the same, nor disturb the Seneca Nation, nor any of the Six Nations, or their Indian friends residing thereon, and united with them, in the free use and enjoyment thereof; but it shall remain theirs, until they choose to sell the same, to the people of the United States, who have the right to purchase.

ARTICLE 4. The United States have thus described and acknowledged what lands belong to the Oneidas, Onondagas, Cayugas and Senecas, and engaged never to claim the same, nor disturb them, or any of the Six Nations, or their Indian friends residing thereon, and united with them, in the free use and enjoyment thereof; now, the Six Nations, and each of them, hereby engage that they will never claim any other lands, within the boundaries of the United States, nor ever disturb the people of the United States in the free use and enjoyment thereof.

ARTICLE 5. The Seneca Nation, all others of the Six Nations concurring cede to the United States the right of making a wagon road from Fort Schlosser to Lake Erie, as far south as Buffalo Creek; and the people of the United States shall have the free and undisturbed use of this road for the purposes of traveling and transportation. And the Six Nations and each of them, will forever allow to the people of the United States, a free passage through their lands, and the free use of the harbors and rivers adjoining and within their respective tracts of land, for the passing and securing of vessels and boats, and liberty to land their cargoes, where necessary, for their safety.

ARTICLE 6. In consideration of the peace and friendship hereby established, and the engagements entered into by the Six Nation; and because the United States desire, with humanity and kindness, to contribute to their comfortable support; and to render the peace and friendship hereby established strong and perpetual, the United States now deliver to the Six Nations, and the Indians of the other nations residing among them, a quantity of goods, of the value of ten thousand dollars. And for the same considerations, and with a view to promote the future welfare of the Six Nations, and of their Indian friends aforesaid, the United States will add the sum of three thousand dollars to the one thousand five hundred dollars heretofore allowed to them by an article ratified by the President, on the twenty-third day of April, 1792, making in the whole four thousand five hundred dollars; which shall be expended yearly, forever, in purchasing clothing, domestic animals, implements of husbandry, and other utensils, suited to their circumstances, and in compensating useful artificers, who shall reside with or near them, and be employed for their benefit. The immediate application of the whole annual allowance now stipulated, to be made by the superintendent, appointed by the President, for the affairs of the Six Nations, and their Indian friends aforesaid.

ARTICLE 7. Lest the firm and friendship now established should be interrupted by the misconduct of individuals, the United States and the Six Nations agree, that for injuries done by individuals, on either side, no private revenge or retaliation shall take place; but, instead thereof, complaint shall be made by the party injured, to the other; by the Six Nations or any of them, to the President of the United States, or the superintendent by him appointed; and by the superintendent, or any other person appointed by the President, to the principal chiefs of the Six Nations, or of the Nation to which the offender belongs; and such prudent measures shall then be pursued, as shall be necessary to preserve the peace and friendship unbroken, until the Legislature (or Great Council) of the United States shall make other equitable provision for that purpose.

NOTE. It is clearly understood by the parties to this treaty, that the annuity, stipulated in the sixth article, is to be applied to the benefit of such of the Six Nations, and of their Indian friends united with them, as aforesaid, as do or shall reside within the boundaries of the United States; for the United States does not interfere with nations, tribes or families of Indians, elsewhere resident.

IN WITNESS WHEREOF, the said Timothy Pickering, and the sachems and war chiefs of the said Six Nations, have hereunto set their hands and seals.

Done at Canandaigua, in the State of New York, in the eleventh day of November, in the year one thousand seven hundred and ninety-four.

TIMOTHY PICKERING

WITNESSES   INTERPRETERS

Israel Chapin   Horatio Jones
Wm. Shepard Jun'r   Joseph Smith
James Smedley   Jasper Parrish
John Wickham   Henry Abeele
Augustus Porter
James H. Garnsey
Wm. Ewing
Israel Chapin, Jun'r

Signed by fifty-nine Sachems and War Chiefs of the Six Nations, including: Handsome Lake, Captain Key, Woods on Fire, Fish Carrier, Farmer's Brother or Nicholas Kusick, Red Jacket, Two Skies Of A Length, Broken Axe, Open The Way or Handsome Lake, Heap Of Dogs, Half Town or Jake Stroud, Stinking Fish, Cornplanter or Captain Prantup, and Green Grasshopper or Big Sky or Little Billy.

NOTES

Notes to the Prologue

1. William Tilden Stauffer, "The Sugarloaf Massacre." *Annals of the Sugarloaf Historical Association, Volume I.* (Hazleton, Pennsylvania: Sugarloaf Historical Association, 1934), 21.

2. George R. Beyer, *Guide to the State Historical Markers of Pennsylvania.* (Harrisburg, Pennsylvania: Pennsylvania Historical and Museum Commission, 1991), 196.

3. Joseph R. Fischer, *A Well-Executed Failure: The Sullivan Campaign Against the Iroquois, July-September 1779.* (Columbia, South Carolina: University of South Carolina Press, 1997), 7.

4. Peter Farb, *Man's Rise to Civilization As Shown By The Indians of North America From Primeval Times To The Coming Of The Industrial State.* (New York: E.P. Dutton & Company, Inc., 1968), 95.

5. Fischer, 195.

6. Barbara Graymont, *The Iroquois in the American Revolution.* (Syracuse, New York: Syracuse University Press, 1972), 240.

7. Ed Conrad, "Klader's Mission Ended in Carnage." *Hazleton Standard-Speaker*, September 6, 1991, A-7.

Notes to Chapter One

On The Warpath: 1780

1. Graymont, 229.

2. C. Hale Sipe, *The Indian Chiefs of Pennsylvania*. (Lewisburg, Pennsylvania: Wennawoods, 1998), 516.

3. C. Hale Sipe, *The Indian Wars of Pennsylvania*. (Lewisburg, Pennsylvania: Wennawoods, 1998), 613.

4. Ibid., 626.

5. Sipe, *The Indian Chiefs of Pennsylvania*, 514.

6. Graymont, 237.

Notes to Chapter Two

Van Etten's Command

1. Lila Van Etten Huddy, "The Van Etten Family." *(Paper presented to the Monroe County Historical Society, Stroudsburg, Pennsylvania, January 15, 1925)*, 8.

2. Ibid., 9.

3. Ibid.

4. John B. Linn and William H. Egle, *Pennsylvania Archives, Second Series, Volume XIV*. (Harrisburg, Pennsylvania: Clarence M. Busch, 1896), 593.

5. Charles Rhoads Roberts, "Pennsylvania Germans and the Revolution." *Annals of the Sugarloaf Historical Association, Volume II*. (Hazleton, Pennsylvania: Sugarloaf Historical Association, 1935), 10.

Notes to Chapter Three

Klader's Detachment

1. Oscar Jewell Harvey and Ernest Gray Smith, *A History of Wilkes-Barre, Luzerne County, Pennsylvania, Volume III*. (Wilkes-Barre, Pennsylvania: Privately Printed, 1927), 1256.

2. Charles Rhoads Roberts, Reverend John Baer Stoudt, Reverend Thomas H. Krick and William J. Dietrich, *History of Lehigh County, Pennsylvania and a Genealogical and Biographical Record of its Families, Volume I*. (Allentown, Pennsylvania: Lehigh Valley, 1914), 155.

3. Paul A. W. Wallace, *Indian Paths of Pennsylvania*. (Harrisburg, Pennsylvania: The Pennsylvania Historical and Museum Commission, 1965), 89.

4. Harvey and Smith, 1256.

5. Jay L. Glickman, *Painted in Blood: Remember Wyoming! America's First Civil War*. (Cody, Wyoming: Affiliated Writers of America, 1997), 147.

Notes to Chapter Four

The Shadow of Death, September 11, 1780

1. Stauffer, "The Sugarloaf Massacre," 21.

2. Donald Kerry Klinefelter, *The Hellers of Sugarloaf.* (Millersburg, Pennsylvania: Privately Printed, 1991), 7.

3. H. C. Bradsby, *History of Luzerne County, Pennsylvania, with Biographical Selections.* (Chicago: S. B. Nelson, 1893), 202.

4. Graymont, 204.

5. Bradsby, 200.

6. George P. Donehoo, *Indian Villages and Place Names In Pennsylvania.* (Baltimore, Gateway, 1977), 119.

7. Ibid.

Notes to Chapter Five

Balliet's Detail

1. Charles Miner, *History of Wyoming, In a Series of Letters from Charles Miner to his son William Penn Miner, Esquire.* (Philadelphia: J. Crissy, 1845), 287.

2. William L. Stone, *Life of Joseph Brant-Thayendanegea: Including the Border Wars of the American Revolution and Sketches of the Indian Campaigns of Generals Harmar, St. Clair, and Wayne.* (New York: Alexander V. Blake, 1838), 230, 231.

3. Harvey and Smith, 1257.

4. Ibid.

5. Reverend William M. Beauchamp, *Iroquois Folk Lore Gathered from the Six Nations of New York.* (Port Washington, New York: Ira J. Friedman, 1865), 236.

6. Bradsby, 202.

7. Harvey and Smith, 1258.

8. Ibid.

9. Ibid.

Notes to Chapter Six

Frontier Endgame: 1781-1783

1. Graymont, 245.

2. Sipe, *The Indian Chiefs of Pennsylvania,* 517.

3. Graymont, 245..

4. Sipe, *The Indian Wars of Pennsylvania,* 617.

5. Graymont, 253.

6. Ibid., 258.

Notes to Chapter Seven

Turnips and Venison

1. Klinefelter, 7.

2. Ibid., 8.

3. Drums Lions Club, *Two Hundred Years of Progress: Butler Township, 1784-1984.* (Drums, Pennsylvania: Keystone Job Corps Center, 1984), 7.

Notes to the Epilogue

1. Roberts, Stoudt, Krick, and Dietrich, 158.

2. Ibid.

3. Stauffer, "The Sugarloaf Massacre," 22.

BIBLIOGRAPHY

Amory, Thomas C. *The Military Services and Public Life of Major-General John Sullivan of the American Revolutionary Army.* Boston: Wiggin and Lunt, 1868.

Beauchamp, Rev. William M. *Iroquois Folk Lore Gathered from The Six Nations of New York.* Port Washington, New York: Ira J. Friedman Inc., 1965.

Beauchamp, Rev. William M. *A History of The New York Iroquois Now Commonly Called the Six Nations.* Port Washington, New York: Ira J. Friedman, Inc., 1968.

Beyer, George R. *Guide to the State Historical Markers of Pennsylvania.* Harrisburg, Pennsylvania: Pennsylvania Historical and Museum Commission, 1991.

Bigelow, Mrs. John L. and Mrs. E. B. Mulligan, Jr., eds. *Let Freedom Ring: Being a Brief History of Conyngham Borough and Sugarloaf Township in Luzerne County, Pennsylvania.* Conyngham, Pennsylvania: Conyngham-Sugarloaf Bicentennial Commission, 1976.

Bradsby, H. C., ed. *History of Luzerne County, Pennsylvania, with Biographical Selections.* Chicago: S. B. Nelson, 1893.

Christopher, Carl. "Rooted in Blood." *Hazleton Standard-Speaker*, September 6, 1991.

Clader, Milo Daniel. "The Klader Family." *Annals of the Sugarloaf Historical Association, Vol. I.* Hazleton, Pennsylvania: Sugarloaf Historical Association, 1934.

Conrad, Ed. "Klader's Mission Ended in Carnage." *Hazleton Standard-Speaker*, September 6, 1991.

Cruikshank, Ernest. *The Story of Butler's Rangers and the Settlement of Niagara.* Welland, Ontario: Tribune Printing House, 1893.

Donehoo, George P. *Indian Villages and Place Names in Pennsylvania.* Baltimore: Gateway Press, Inc., 1977.

"Dramatic Recital of Patriot Sacrifice." *Sunday Independent,* September 10, 1933.

Drums Lions Club. *Two Hundred Years of Progress: Butler Township, 1784-1984.* Drums, Pennsylvania: Keystone Job Corps Center, 1984.

Farb, Peter. *Man's Rise to Civilization as Shown by the Indians of North America from Primeval Times to the Coming of the Industrial State.* New York: E. P. Dutton & Company, Inc., 1968.

Fink, Margaret. *Christ Church United Church of Christ, 1809-1984.* Conyngham, Pennsylvania: Privately Printed, 1984.

Fischer, Joseph R. *A Well-Executed Failure: The Sullivan Campaign Against The Iroquois, July-September 1779.* Columbia, South Carolina: University of South Carolina Press, 1997.

Glickman, Jay L. *Painted in Blood: Remember Wyoming! America's First Civil War.* Cody, Wyoming: Affiliated Writers of America, Inc., 1997.

Godcharles, Frederic A. *Daily Stories of Pennsylvania.* Milton, Pennsylvania: Privately Printed, 1924.

Graymont, Barbara. *The Iroquois in the American Revolution.* Syracuse, New York: Syracuse University Press, 1972.

Harvey, Oscar Jewell and Ernest Gray Smith. *A History of Wilkes-Barre, Luzerne County, Pennsylvania, Vol. III.* Wilkes-Barre, Pennsylvania: Privately Printed, 1927.

Huddy, Lila Van Etten. "The Van Etten Family." *Paper Presented to the Monroe County Historical Society, Stroudsburg, Pennsylvania, January 15, 1925.*

Klinefelter, Donald Kerry. *The Hellers of Sugarloaf.* Millersburg, Pennsylvania: Privately Printed, 1991.

Linn, John B. and William H. Egle, eds. *Pennsylvania Archives, Second Series, Vol, XIV.* Harrisburg, Pennsylvania: Clarence M. Busch, State Printer of Pennsylvania, 1896.

Lydekker, John Wolfe. *The Faithful Mohawks.* Port Washington, New York: Ira J. Friedman, Inc., 1968.

Martens, Henry C. *Conyngham, Pennsylvania: A Brief History of the Area up to 1966 with Particular Reference to the History of Christ Lutheran Church.* New Hartford, New York: Privately Printed, 1967.

Mathews, Alfred. *History of Wayne, Pike and Monroe Counties, Pennsylvania.* Philadelphia: R. T. Peck and Company, 1886.

Miner, Charles. *History of Wyoming, In a Series of Letters, from Charles Miner to his son William Penn Miner, Esquire.* Philadelphia: J. Crissy, 1845.

Mintz, Max M. *Seeds of Empire: The American Revolutionary Conquest of the Iroquois.* New York: New York University Press, 1999.

Montgomery, Thomas Lynch, ed. *Report of the Commission to Locate the Site of the Frontier Forts of Pennsylvania, Vol. I.* Harrisburg, Pennsylvania: William Stanley Ray, State Printer, 1916.

Munsell, W. W. *History of Luzerne, Lackawanna and Wyoming Counties, Pennsylvania, with Biographical Sketches of Some of their Prominent Men and Pioneers.* New York: W. W. Munsell & Company, 1880.

"Old Time Letter About Massacre." *Hazleton Standard-Sentinel*, July 21, 1933.

Pearce, Stewart. *Annals of Luzerne County; a record of Interesting Events, Traditions, and Anecdotes from the First Settlement at Wyoming to 1860*. Philadelphia: J. B. Lippincott & Company, 1860.

Richards, Henry M. *The Pennsylvania-German in the Revolutionary War, 1775-1783*. Baltimore: Genealogical Publishing Company, Inc., 1978.

Roberts, Charles Rhoads, Rev. John Baer Stoudt, Rev. Thomas H. Krick and William J. Dietrich. *History of Lehigh County, Pennsylvania and a Genealogical and Biographical Record of its Families, Vol. I*. Allentown, Pennsylvania: Lehigh Valley Publishing Company, Ltd., 1914.

Roberts, Charles Rhoads. "Pennsylvania Germans and the Revolution." *Annals of the Sugarloaf Historical Association, Vol. II*. Hazleton, Pennsylvania: Sugarloaf Historical Association, 1935.

Roslevich, John Jr. "Indians, Tories Massacred Continentals at Sugarloaf Spring 190 Years Ago Today." *Hazleton Standard-Speaker*, September 11, 1970.

Sipe, C. Hale. *The Indian Chiefs of Pennsylvania*. Lewisburg, Pennsylvania: Wennawoods Publishing, 1998.

Sipe, C. Hale, *The Indian Wars of Pennsylvania*. Lewisburg, Pennsylvania: Wennawoods Publishing, 1998.

Stauffer, William Tilden. "Massacre Story Facts Revealed." *Hazleton Standard-Sentinel*, August 1, 1933.

Stauffer, William Tilden. "Story on Massacre of Capt. Klader's Company by Indians and Tories close to Present Site of Conyngham Borough." *The Plain Speaker*, July 8, 1932.

Stokes, John C. "Sugarloaf Massacre." *Hazleton Sentinel*, September, 1866.

Stone, William L. *Life of Joseph Brant-Thayendanegea: Including the Border Wars of the American Revolution and Sketches of the Indian Campaigns of Generals Harmar, St. Clair, and Wayne.* 2 vols. New York: Alexander V. Blake, 1838.

Stone, William L. *The Poetry and History of Wyoming: Containing Campbell's Gertrude, with a Biographical Sketch of the Author, by Washington Irving, and the History of Wyoming, from its Discovery to the Beginning of the Present Century.* New York: Wiley and Putnam, 1841.

"Sugarloaf Massacre 200 Years Ago." *Hazleton Standard-Speaker*, September 12, 1980.

"Sugarloaf Monument Marks Site Where Indians and Tories Butchered Whole Company of Revolutionary Soldiers." *Hazleton Plain Speaker*, August 26, 1941.

Swiggett, Howard. *War Out of Niagara: Walter Butler and the Tory Rangers.* Port Washington, New York: Ira J. Friedman, Inc., 1933.

"The Sugarloaf Massacre." *Hazleton Standard-Speaker*, September 10, 1971.

Wallace, Anthony F. C. *The Death and Rebirth of the Seneca.* New York: Alfred A. Knopf, Inc., 1970.

Wallace, Paul A. W. *Indian Paths of Pennsylvania.* Harrisburg, Pennsylvania: The Pennsylvania Historical and Museum Commission, 1965.

Whelan, Frank. "13 Northampton County Militiamen Lost Their Scalps in Indian, Tory Ambush, Sugarloaf Massacre." *Allentown Morning Call*, August 3, 1986.

INDEX

A

Abeele, Henry, 86
Adams, Samuel, 71
Albany (NY), 51
Allen, Richard, 71
Allentown (PA)
Altmiller, J. E., 74
American Revolution, 7, 9,
    10, 12, 13, 29, 64, 66, 69,
    75, 76
Amory, Thomas C., 12
Apler, Pvt. Peter, 80
Arndt, Pvt. Jacob, 7, 39, 81

B

Bald Eagle Creek, 63
Balliet, John, 69
Balliet, Lt. Col. Stephen, 8,
    47-49, 69, 77, 78
Ballston (NY), 51
Beacraft, Benjamin, 22
Beatty, Lt. 48
Beaver Creek, 34
Bennet, Thomas, 18, 19
Berwick (PA), 42
Bethlehem (PA), 28
Big Sky,
    see Green Grasshopper.
Big Tree,
    see Carondowanen.
Bishop, Pvt. Antony, 82
Bitten, Pvt. Philip, 27, 81
Black Creek, 37

Blaine, Col, Ephraim, 46-48,
    51
Bloomsburg (PA), 33, 62
Blue Mountain, 14, 20, 25, 31
Bond, Corp. Samuel, 7, 39,
    79
Bonin, John H., 75
Braddock, Gen. Edward, 42
Brady, Capt. Samuel, 61
Brant, Joseph,
    see Thayendanegea.
Broad Mountain, 20, 33, 34
Broken Axe, 86
Brown, Lt., 61
Brunthaver, Pvt. Adam, 28,
    82
Buck Mountain, 8, 14, 37, 39,
    45, 69, 76
Bucks County (PA), 27
Buffalo Creek, 84
Bunker Hill, Battle of, 9, 28
Bureau Brothers, 74
Burgoyne, Gen. John, 12
Bush, Ensign Henry, 79
Busz, Anna Catherine, 28
Butler, Col. Walter, 64
Butler, Col. Zebulon, 46, 50,
    51, 64
Butler's Rangers, 12, 22, 31,
    51, 52, 173
Byberry (PA), 20, 21

C

Campbell, Capt., 62
Canada, 21, 27, 41, 51

Canajoharie District, 22, 26
Canandaigua, Treaty of, 66, 83-86
Carbon County (PA), 20
Carleton, Gen. Sir Guy, 20, 65
Carondowanen, 41
Catawbas, 41
Catawissa, 42
Cayuga Lake, 11
Cayugas, 11, 17, 51, 83-86
Chapin, Israel, 86
Chapin, Israel, Jr. 86,
Chapman, Asa, 65, 66
Chemung (NY), 40
Cherry Valley (NY), 10, 62
Chesapeake Bay, 14
Chew Tobacco, 61
Chillisquaque Creek, 32
Clader, Milo Daniel, 75
Clark, Gen., 63
Clutter, Pvt. Casper, 82
Coans, Pvt. Peter Tubalt, 39, 45, 48, 74, 80
Collens, Pvt. Jacob, 81
Columbia County (PA), 70
Continental Army, 10, 11, 46
Continental Congress, 11
Conyngham (PA), 7, 8, 14
Conyngham, Redmond, 71
Cornplanter, 51, 86
Cornwallis, Gen. Lord Charles, 64
Craig, Capt. Thomas, 27, 28
Cramer, Lt., 62
Crawford, Col. William, 65
Cret, Paul, 74
Croom, Pvt. Peter, 7, 39, 81

Cryder, Pvt. Jacob, 80
Crysler, Lt. Adam, 64

D

Daniel, Pvt. Peter, 82
Davis, Pvt. Henry, 39, 69, 81
Davis, Philip, 32
Dayly, Pvt. John, 82
Dearborn, Lt. Henry, 34
Decker, Daniel, 26
Deily, Philip, 28
Delawares, 13, 14, 17, 40, 61
Delaware Valley, 25, 62
Deserontyon, Capt. John, 61, 65
Devoor, Pvt. Cornelius, 82
Dodson, Abigail, 20, 73, 75
Dodson, Samuel, 20
Dorrance, Frances, 74
Drum, George, 69-71
Durham boats, 71

E

Easterday, George, 69
Easton (PA), 10, 14, 34
Emerson, Ralph Waldo, 76
Engel, Susanna, 27
Everhart, Sgt. Frederick, 79
Ewing, William, 86

F

Farmer's Brother,
    see Fish Carrier.
Finger Lakes, 10
Fischer, Joseph R., 13

Fisher, Joseph, 73
Fish Carrier, 86
Fish Hook, 18
Fish, Lt. John, 79
Five Nations,
  see Iroquois.
Forseman, Hugh, 47, 50, 51
Fort Allen, 14, 20, 31, 32, 33,
  46, 47, 48, 64, 69
Fort Ann, 51
Fort Augusta, 8, 25, 32, 51,
  62
Fort Coeur du Lac, 21
Fort Freeland, 32
Fort George, 51
Fort Hamilton, 25
Fort Herkimer, 63
Fort Hyndshaw, 25
Fort Jenkins, 33, 34, 39, 41,
  46, 62
Fort McClure, 62
Fort Montgomery,
  see Fort Rice.
Fort Muncy, 62, 63
Fort Niagara, 12, 17, 18, 22,
  34, 39, 40, 46, 48, 51, 52,
  61-64, 74, 84
Fort Norris, 31
Fort Penn, 25, 26, 31, 82
Fort Pitt, 61, 63
Fort Rice, 32, 33, 41, 46
Fort Schlosser, 84
Fort Schoharie, 18, 64
Fort Stanwix, 22, 63
Fort Wyoming, 8, 19, 31, 37,
  46, 50-52
France, 41
France, Pvt. Daniel, 80

France, Pvt. Henry, 82
Franklin, Benjamin, 25
Franklin, Capt. John, 19
French and Indian War, 25,
  31

G

Gable, Sgt. Joseph, 79, 81
Ganaghsaraga Creek, 64
Gangawere, Pvt. George, 27,
  31, 80
Gangawere, Pvt, Jacob, 27
Garnsey, James H. 86
Gay, Corp. Thomas, 79
Genesee River, 10, 11, 46, 63
George, Pvt. Philip, 7, 39, 81
Giger, Col., 47, 77, 78
Gilbert, Abner, 20
Gilbert, Benjamin, Sr., 20, 21
Gilbert, Benjamin, Jr., 20
Gilbert, Elizabeth, 20, 21
Gilbert, Jesse, 20
Gilbert, John, 20
Gilbert, Joseph, 20
Gilbert, Rebecca, 20
Gilbert, Sarah, 20
Glickman, Jay L., 12
Gnadenhuetten (PA), 31, 32,
  64, 77
Gonzales, Maria, 26
Graymont, Barbara, 13
Gray, William, 14
Great Britain, 9, 11, 12, 20,
  22, 32, 40, 41, 47, 48, 50,
  52, 63-66, 73, 78, 84
"Great Island" (PA), 63
Great Plains, 9

"Great Swamp," 34
Green Grasshopper, 86
Grove, Michael, 62
"Grove Party," 62
Grove, Peter, 62

H

Hain, Pvt. John, 82
"Hair Buyer," 18
Haldimand, Gen., 65
Half Town, 86
Haller, Pvt. Christian, 80
Hamilton, Gen. Henry, 18
Hammond, Lebbeus, 18, 19
Hand, Gen. Edward, 40
Handsome Lake, 86
Hanover (PA), 65
Harper, Capt. Alexander, 18
Harper, Col. John, 22
Harrigar, Andrew, 20
Harvey, Benjamin, 45
"Haselschwamp," 14, 34, 37
Haun, Pvt. John, 81
Hazle Creek, 34, 37
Hazleton Liberty Band, 74,
    75
Hazleton (PA), 8, 37
"Hazleton Sentinel," 8, 73
Heap of Dogs, 86
Hecker, Corp. Adam, 27
Hecker, Frederick Christian,
    27
Hecker, John Wigand, 27
Hecker, Rev. John Egidius,
    27
Heller, E. Foster, 74
Heller, John Deiter, 69

Hellet, Sgt. Samuel, 79
Henritzy, George S., 74
Heter, Pvt. George, 81
Heter, Pvt. Bond, 82
Hewe, Pvt. Thomas, 82
Hiakatoo, 18, 49
Hicker, Corp. Adam, 79
Hikman, Pvt. George, 80
Hill, David, 22, 61
Hill, Capt. Isaac, 65
Hilliard, Blanch Ernst, 75
Hojiagede, 17
Holmes, Corp. Lewis, 79
Hornick, Joseph, 74, 75
Hough, Chief Philip, 61
Houser, Pvt. Jacob, 80
Hubley, Lt. Col. Adam, 40
Huddy, Lila Van Etten, 26
Huff, Pvt. Solomon, 82
Hung Face, Chief, 51
Hunsinger, Bernard, 70
Hunter, Robert,
    see Carondowanen.
Hunter, Col. Samuel, 19, 31,
    32, 62

I

Ireland, 11
Iroquois, 7, 10-13, 17, 41, 48,
    62, 64, 66, 83-86
Jameson, Benjamin, 65, 66
Jameson, John, 65, 66
Jemison, Mary, 18, 49
Jenkins, Lt. John, Jr., 46, 52
Jim Thorpe (PA),
    see Mauch Chunk, (PA).
Johnson, Col. Guy, 12, 13, 17

Johnson, Sir John, 21, 51
Johnson, Sir William, 75
Johnston, Lt. William, 33, 37,
    73
Johnston, Sgt. Thomas, 74
Johnstown (NY), 22
Jones, Horatio, 86

K

Karaghqunty, David, 61
Kelly, Col. John, 32
Kern, Lt. Col., 28, 31, 47, 77,
    78
Key, Capt., 86
Kirkland, Rev. Samuel, 10,
    22
Kishacoquillas Creek, 42
Klader, Capt. Daniel, 7, 8, 13,
    27-29, 31-34, 37-43, 45-
    47, 50, 69, 72-76
Klader, Capt. Jacob, 29, 75
Klader, Christiana, 27
Klader, Pvt. Abraham, 7, 8,
    27, 29, 39, 80
Klader, Valentine, 27, 28
Klenner, Rev. T., 71
Knapsnyder, Pvt. John, 28, 80
Kouts, Pvt. John, 7, 39, 80
Kowler, Pvt. Coanrode, 80
Kusick, Nicholas,
    see Fish Carrier.

L

Lake Erie, 84
Lake Ontario, 21, 83, 84
Lasher, Pvt. Peter, 80

Lehigh Path, 33
Lehigh River, 64
Lehigh Valley, 33
Little Beard, Chief, 17
Little Billy,
    see Green Grasshopper.
Little Nescopeck Creek, 7, 9,
    14, 15, 22, 37-43, 45, 49,
    71, 76
Lochry, Col. Archibald, 61,
    63
Lock Haven (PA), 63
Lung, Pvt. Adam, 81
Luzerne County (PA), 65
Lycoming County (PA), 63
Lyn, Pvt. John, 81

M

MacDonald, Capt. John, 32
Mack, Hackwelder, 37
Mahoning Creek, 40, 73
Mahoning Mountain, 20
"Manifest Destiny," 10
Mann, Rev. John, 71
Markle, Marion Vaughn, 75
Massachusetts, 50
Mauch Chunk (PA), 33
Mauch Chunk Ridge, 20, 33
McCoy, Pvt. Peter, 81
McDole, Pvt. Daniel, 80
McDonnell, Capt. John, 22
McGraw, Pvt. James, 7, 30,
    82
Miamis, 41
Miller, Christian, 69, 70
Miller, Pvt. Lawrence, 80
Milton (PA), 32

Miner, Charles, 9
Mintz, Max M., 13
Mississippi River, 42
Mohawk River, 11, 21, 51,
    62, 64, 65
Mohawks, 11, 17
Montgomery, John, 32
Montour, Andrew, 41, 42
Montour, Lewis, 41
Montour, Madame, 41, 75
Montour, Margaret, 41
Montour, Robert, 41
Montour, Roland, 7, 8, 11,
    18, 21, 33, 34, 37-43, 45,
    48, 49
Montour's Island (PA), 42
Montreal, 21, 41
Moravians, 31, 37, 64, 65
Morgan, Pvt. John, 82
Morhart, Pvt. John, 80
Mourer, Pvt. Andrew, 81
Mowery, Andrew, 69
Myer, Pvt. Andrew, 81
Myer, Lt. John, 8, 34, 39, 45,
    46, 49, 74, 77-79
Myer, Pvt. John, 80

N

Nanticokes, 17
Nanticoke Trail, 14
Neely, Pvt. Paul, 7, 28, 39, 81
Neligh, Henry, 28
Nesquehoning Creek, 33
Nescopeck Creek, 37, 39, 49,
    71
Nescopeck Mountain, 14, 39,
    45

Nescopeck Trail, 14, 20, 34,
    37, 45
Netherlands, 26
New Hampshire, 10
New Jersey, 25, 50
New York, 10, 17, 21, 26, 46,
    50-52, 61, 64, 83
Nicholas, Pvt. Voluntine, 80
Northampton County (PA), 7
Novotnie, George, 74, 75

O

Ohio, 61
Ohio River, 62
Oneida Lake, 11, 66
Oneidas, 11, 22, 41, 51, 64,
    83-86
Onondaga River, 11
Onondagas, 11, 17, 22, 42,
    83-86
Open The Way,
    see Handsome Lake.
Oswego (NY), 51, 64, 65

P

Pack, Pvt. Leonard, 80
Parrish, Jasper, 86
Peart, Benjamin, 20
Peart, Elizabeth, 20
Peart, infant, 20
Peart, Thomas, 20
Penn, Governor John, 25
Pennsylvania, 7-14, 17-23,
    40, 45, 50, 52, 61, 65, 75
Pennsylvania Germans, 26,
    29, 69, 70, 71

Phelps, Oliver, 83, 84
Philadelphia, 20, 41, 46, 51
Pickering, Timothy, 83-86
Pigg, Pvt. George, 80
Pike, Abraham, 19
Pittsburgh (PA), 42
Pocono Mountains, 10, 31
Porter, Augustus, 86
Prantup, Capt.,
  see Cornplanter.
Price, Sgt. George, 79
Purdy, Col., 32

Q

Quackack, Chief, 63
Quakake Creek, 20, 34
Quakers, 20
Queen Esther, 41, 42, 75
Quick, Pvt. Peter, 82

R

Red Jacket, Chief, 86
Reed, Joseph, 8, 19, 20, 48,
  50, 77, 78
Reeser, Pvt. Paul, 81
Renhart, Pvt. George Peter, 7,
  39, 81
Revolutionary War, see
  American Revolution.
Rice, Charles H., 74
Rice, Capt. John, 75
Ripsher, Pvt. George, 80
Rittenhouse, David,70
Rittenhouse, William, 70
Robenholt, Pvt. John, 80
Roberts, Charles Rhoads, 73

Rogers, Jonah, 19
Ross, Maj. John, 64
Roth, Rev. Allen H., 74
Row, Pvt. Jacob, 7, 39, 82
"Royal Yorkers," 51
Roy, Col. Samuel, 49
Rule, Dr. James N., 75

S

Sack, Pvt. John, 80
Sagwarithra, 51
Saratoga, Battle of, 9, 40
Sayenqueraghta, 51, 65
scalps, 9, 18, 20
Scoby, Ensign James, 34, 39,
  45, 46, 48, 49, 74, 79
Scotch Valley,
  see Sugarloaf Valley.
Senecas, 7, 11, 15, 17, 33, 34,
  37-43, 48, 63, 74, 83-86
"Shades of Death," 34
Shamokin (PA), 40, 62, 69
Shannon, Lt. Gov. Edward
  C., 75
Shawnees, 17
Shawanese Mountain, 46, 52
Shellhammer, Philip Jacob,
  27
Shenesboro (NY), 18
Shepard, William, Jr., 86
Shickler, Frederick, 8
Shilhamer, Pvt. George, 7,
  39, 81
Shilhamer, Pvt. Peter George,
  27, 81
Shinop, Capt., 17, 61
Simonton, Pvt. Peter, 82

Siner, Pvt. Peter, 80
Sinnemahoning Creek, 62
Six Nations,
    see Iroquois.
Smedley, James, 86
Smith, Dr. William H., 45
Smith, Joseph, 86
Smith, Pvt. Abraham, 7, 39,
    81
Smith, Pvt. Daniel, 27, 80
Smith, Pvt. John, 80
Smith, Pvt. John, Jr., 81
Smith, Pvt. Rudolph, 27, 80
Smith, Rudolph, Sr., 27
Snider, Pvt. John, 82
Snyder, Pvt. Baltzer, 7, 39, 81
Snyder, Pvt. Johannes, 81
Snyder, Pvt. Peter, 80
Staudenmeier, Christopher,
    75
Stauffer, William Tilden, 8,
    75, 76
St. Clair, Col., 27
Stewart, William, 47, 51
Stinking Fish, 86
St. Lawrence River, 21
Stokes, John C., 8
Stone Arabia (NY), 51
Stout, Pvt. Job, 80
Stroud, Col. Jacob, 20, 25, 82
Stroud, Jake,
    see Half Town.
Stroudsburg (PA), 25
Sugarloaf Massacre, 7-9, 22,
    26, 28, 29, 40, 52, 66, 73-
    76
Sugarloaf Mountain, 14, 66,
    70

Sugarloaf Valley, 7, 14, 15,
    31, 32, 37, 46, 66, 69-73,
    76, 77
Sullivan Expedition, 10-17,
    40, 65
Sullivan, Maj. Gen. John, 10,
    12, 34, 52, 75
Summeny, Pvt. Samuel, 28,
    81
Susquehanna River, 10, 14,
    19, 37, 39, 40, 45, 46, 52,
    62, 71, 77

T

Tanaghkewas, 17
Teel, Pvt. Adam, 80
Thayendanegea, 17, 18, 22,
    51, 61, 62, 65
Tippy, Pvt. Uriah, 81
tomahawks, 7, 64
Tories, 7, 8, 10, 17, 22, 31,
    77
Trenton, Battle of, 9
Tryon County (NY), 21, 51
Turney, Lt. John, Sr., 52
Tuscaroras, 22, 51, 61
Tuteloes, 17
Two Skies Of A Length, 86

U

Ulster County (NY), 63
Upson, Asa, 19

V

Valley Forge (PA), 9

Van Campen, Moses, 19, 62, 63
Vandermark, Pvt. Samuel, 80
Van Etten, Anthony, 26
Van Etten, Capt. Johannes (John), 7, 25-29, 31, 79, 82
Van Etten, Catherine, 26
Van Etten, Cornelius, 26
Van Etten, Daniel, 26
Van Etten, Dorothy, 26
Van Etten, Elizabeth, 26
Van Etten, Jacob, 26
Van Etten, James, 26
Van Etten, Johannes, Jr., 26
Van Etten, Magdalena, 26
Van Etten, Manuel, 26
Van Etten, Rymerick, 26
Van Etten, Simeon, 26
Van Etten, Solomon, 26
Van Garden, Pvt. Henry, 82
Van Garden, Pvt. Samuel, 82
Van Sikkle, Pvt. Thomas, 82
Vaudreuil, Gov., 41
Von ZinZendorf, Count Nicholas Ludwig, 37, 42
Vrooman family, 22
Vrooman, Peter, 22

W

Wadhams, Mrs. Raymond L., 74
Wagner Farm, 7
Warren's Bush (NY), 64
Washington, Gen. George, 9, 12, 50, 64, 66, 83-86

Washington's Crossing, 9
Wawarsing (NY), 63
Wayne, Gen. Anthony, 29
Weaver, Anthony, 70
Weaver, Pvt. John, 7, 39, 80
Weiser, Conrad, 42
Weissport (PA), 14
Westbrook, Antje, 25
Westfall, Pvt. Abraham, 70, 82
Wetherstone, Pvt. John, 80
Wever, Pvt. Ballser, 81
Whittemore, Charles P., 12
Wickham, John, 86
Wilkes-Barre (PA), 52, 65
Willett, Col. Marinus, 63, 64, 66
Williamson, Col, David, 65
Williams, Rachael, 26
Wind Gap (PA), 33
Wisner, Pvt. Abraham, 81
Wood, Pvt. Christian, 82
Woodring, Philip, 69
Woodring, Samuel, 71
Woods On Fire, 86
Wounded Knee Massacre, 10, 19
Wyoming Massacre, 13, 14, 25, 40, 41
Wyoming Valley, 9, 13, 17-19, 33, 77

Y

Yerty, Pvt. Michael, 82
Yorktown, Battle of, 9, 64

Z

Zane, Isaac, 33

7847339R0

Made in the USA
Lexington, KY
21 December 2010